TEACHING CHILDREN TO SKI

TEACHING CHILDREN TO SKI

ASBJÖRN FLEMMEN
OLAV GROSVOLD

TRANSLATED BY
MICHAEL BRADY

LEISURE PRESS

NEW YORK

HUMAN KINETICS

CHAMPAIGN, ILLINOIS

A publication of Human Kinetics Publishers, Inc.,
Box 5076, Champaign, Illinois 61820
and Leisure Press,
597 Fifth Ave., New York, New York 10017
Original title Ski og Skoyter, Copyright © 1980,
Universitetsforlaget, Olso
Copyright © 1982 by Asbjorn Flemmen, Olav Grosvold and Michael Brady.
All rights reserved. Printed in the U.S.A.

- Published 1983.
ISBN 88011-165-8
Library of Congress No. 83-80708

Cover Design: Brian Groppe
Drawings: Sturla Kaasa
Book Production: H&C Custom Publishing Co., Inc.,
Emeryville, California

CONTENTS

ABOUT THE AUTHORS

Asbjörn Flemmen and Olav Grosvold together have over a half a century of ski instructing experience, the bulk of it teaching children to ski. They are both career teachers, and have taught physical education and related subjects at all levels, from primary schools through teacher training colleges and the Norwegian College of Physical Education and Sport. They have both long been involved in the work of the Skiing in Schools Committee of *Interski,* the International Ski Instruction Association. Author Flemmen now lives in Volda, Norway, and is on the physical education faculty of the teacher training college there, teaching courses at all levels, from those for preschool teachers to those for athletic specialists. Author Grosvold is the principal of Adult Education in Asker, Norway, and a member of the Board of Examiners of The Norwegian Ski School.

PREFACE

Legend has it that Norwegians are born shod with skis. The fact behind the legend is that in the country where skiing was born, Norwegians have traditionally believed that skiing, like walking, is something instinctive. It's first experienced at home and then developed under the guidance of one's parents.

But the bucolic good old days are gone forever, and skiing now covers a far broader range of recreational and sporting activities than did its utilitarian parent, skiing as a means of wintertime transportation. So now it's only natural for Norwegians, like the people of other skiing countries, to regard skiing as an art to be learned.

This is a book on that type of learning. It's aim is to impart skiing skills to children, from tots to preteens. The original Norwegian edition was intended primarily to aid preschool and grade-school recreation and physical education teachers, yet the approach was deliberately devoid of any tie to school or class situations. It is as adaptable to informal instruction by parents or friends, community recreation programs, or instruction in clubs, as it is to school recreation or ski area class situations. It might be called a natural approach.

Part of the natural approach is a reversal of what is emphasized in most conventional schemes and systems of teaching skiing: the focus is on learning by the pupil instead of on teaching by the instructor. The natural approach is based on the belief that any child can develop skiing talents if given the chance to do so in suitable surroundings. Skiing is not a special adult activity into which children can be thrust and grow into, but rather a circumstance that should be part of their expanding world. The approach of making skiing special and different often does little more than make it seem complicated and demanding, which may lead children to become avid non-skiers. And that's worse than if they had not been exposed to snow and skiing at all.

Oslo, Norway, December 1982

Asbjörn Flemmen
Olav Grosvold
Michael Brady

INTRODUCTION

Much to the chagrin of many an adult skiing neophyte, a child — almost any child — is a "born skier." For children, skis and snow are just another form of play, another way to explore their rapidly expanding world.

In on-snow play children can acquire skiing skills as rapidly as they pick up other skills off the snow. There are many reasons for the speed with which kids learn to ski — and we'll mention a few of them later — but kids learn quickly primarily because they have few of the adult hangups about being beginners, seeming foolish, falling, impressing, doing well the first time out, or impressing one's friends. Most of the time, they just want to enjoy themselves.

This is why you, as a parent or a teacher, don't have to be the best skier around to successfully teach children to ski. In fact, in Norway, where almost all children learn to ski, some of the best adult instructors for children are themselves average skiers. What's most important — the very key to their success in teaching children — is that they arrange learning situations that motivate, continually encourage their pupils, and spend time having good contact with children on skis.

In fact, children seldom try to copy adults exactly, simply because they can't. They view the world in their own special way. Their thoughts differ from those of adults; and their bodies and the ways in which they move are different. If you doubt that this is so, think of falling, rolling around in the snow, getting up, and falling again as often as kids do, in the positions they get into. Chances are if you tried it you would end up with dislocations if not worse. Children simply aren't terribly concerned with form or how they appear on skis, but rather with how effective they are and with what they can experience in skiing.

Even the most proficient kids on skis look like-well, proficient kids on skis. There's no escaping that fact. Skiing-wise, children simply are not small adults; they are different. That's why the illustrations in this book were drawn from high-speed motion pictures of children skiing. What you see here is what you can expect of your average pupils. And they can easily identify with the drawings of well-executed maneuvers if you show them the book. Also, of you are new to the art of teaching kids to ski, the illustrations of the maneuvers in the following chapters will show you what awaits you out on the snow; the development of a childlike proficiency that can grow. So it's always best to resist the temptation to tamper with form and let the youngsters ski naturally. If you do, you may be amazed by the results.

Books on skiing often contain incredibly involved descriptions of maneuvers, and ski magazine articles thrive on the minute details of the sport. Understanding the details of a maneuver is fine for you, the teacher. But perhaps the best single piece of advice we can give to anyone teaching children to ski is **avoid making it technical for them.** Detailed explanations, if comprehended, are almost lost on children for several reasons. First, especially for pre-schoolers, they may still be grappling with remembering adult concepts such as right, left, up, down, in, out and so on, and over-instructing ruins their fun. Second, as anyone who has ever verbally instructed kids can attest, their attention span is short, and becomes shorter if something else interesting is nearby — and out on the snow there is something else interesting nearby — skiing.

Kids want action, not talk. The explanations in this book are for you, the instructor, not for your small pupils. Out on the snow the focus should be on the learning of skiing, not the teaching of it. The emphasis should be on the pupils, not the instructor.

About Technique

In skiing, **technique** is a loaded word. It's seldom mentioned without a modifier: **cross-country technique, Alpine technique, French technique** and so on. Its many definitions may be excellent fodder for off-snow bull sessions, but otherwise they mar the learning picture. The chief problem is that technique is frequently misunderstood to be a goal in itself.

My first time on skis.

So we'll define technique in a simple way, the way we use it in this book:

> ### Need produces technique.

This definition jibes with the development of all techniques and with the ways they are naturally learned. For instance, the diagonal stride of cross-country skiing is the result of a development initiated by the desire to ski faster; and the turning of skis with the legs in Alpine skiing resulted from developments initiated by the linking of more rapid turns together. These developments are also the guidelines for the most effective learning pathways: on the flat a skier speeding up will end up in a diagonal stride, and on downhills a skier striving to turn rapidly will use counter-rotation, turning the skis with the legs.

In other words, technique isn't something skiers put on like a change of clothes. Its relation to specific requirements or needs is fundamental and the very cornerstone of learning. As an instructor of a group of pre-schoolers you don't, for instance, tell your skiers that "today we're going to learn the diagonal stride because with it you can ski faster," but rather you construct a situation in which you encourage the skiers to ski faster and simply guide the resultant development of their diagonal strides.

So in this book, **technique** is the result of what skiers do on snow.

Start Simple, Stick to the Basics

There once was only one form of skiing: utilitarian over-snow transport originated in and around the Scandinavian peninsula of northern Europe. Skis and skiing naturally lent themselves to recreation, and then to winter sports. By the early part of this century, when skiing was a healthy four thousand plus years old, different forms of skiing developed, springing out from the common root. **Ski jumping,** emphasizing flight through the air, **Alpine skiing,** emphasizing the downhill aspects of the sport, and **cross-country** or **touring**, emphasizing the covering of distance in terrain, all developed as separate forms of the sport. By the 1970's these three major skiing disciplines had become so specialized that they were thought of by many as separate on-snow sports. And, unfortunately, the trend spread down to lower and lower age groups. But now the gaps separating the three are being bridged, as devotees of one form discover the others. The current **Telemarking** renaissance incorporates cross-country and Alpine skiing, but is really a rediscovery of the joys of the latter sport when it was in its infancy in the 1930's. In the newer parallel Alpine ski races, particularly those of the pro ski circuits, racers are often in the air, jumping off smaller ski jumps as they race. They are combining Alpine slalom racing and ski jumping.

While all this development has been going on, kids have been learning to ski, as they always have. Even if constrained by parents to one form of skiing, they have tried everything as they played on the snow. A kid on

I learned to ski by myself like this . . .

or this,

cross-country skis will race playmates down-hill, and a kid on Alpine skis will skate around a flat or jump over bumps in a downhill, making a game of skiing as it comes.

There's still a common root in all of skiing, especially in skiing for children. Just as a child can do almost anything on foot wearing a single pair of worn sneakers — run, jump, climb trees, dance, hike, paddle a canoe or whatever — a child can, and should, do anything on snow using a single pair of skis of a universal type. Putting kids, particularly kids just learning skiing, into specialized gear of any type only slows their learning of the sport, hampers their enjoyment of it, and, in many cases, prevents them from learning something at which they might have superior capability. It's about as sensible, say, as teaching a pre-school girl to dance by outfitting her in high-heeled shoes and cocktail dress, or teaching a tot to ride a bike by first fitting him with special cycle racing shoes. Equipment cannot produce skills.

No Errors Here

Many stylized schools of skiing instruction have exact views of what's "correct" and what's "in error," or what's "wrong" and what's "right," to use the labels often affixed to pairs of photos or drawings in books and magazine articles.

We view the learning of skiing differently. Children learning to ski are not computers. There's no "correct program" for them, from which the departures are "errors." And besides, as we point out in the beginning of Chapter 3, many of the ostensible "errors" committed by children on skis are actually not errors, but rather very efficient and "correct" ways to ski. The "error" label is often applied when kids depart from the currently held notions of skiing style, but children who do their best at their particular stage of development do not ski "wrong."

Just as kids have problems learning to do anything well, from walking to playing the piano, they may have problems learning to ski well. But with careful guidance, these problems can be overcome. So we think of problems to be overcome as an ongoing learning process rather than errors indicating deviation from some accepted norm. So the word **error** appears only seven times in this book: six times in these three paragraphs and once in their heading, and nowhere else.

Skiing first

This book is divided into two major parts. First, there's what we call just plain, universal **skiing**, where kids should start, with a single set of gear. The goal here is simply a set of skiing skills that will enable children to go anywhere and do anything on skis, within, of course, their range of ability. We like to think of it as a level where kids can be turned loose to go on a ski tour on their own, skiing uphill, downhill, and on flats, jumping and playing as they go.

With these universal and basic skiing skills, children — or their parents — may wish to sharpen specific skills. That's what the second major part of the book is about. Skills for covering flat and uphill terrain are grouped under cross-country in Chapter 2; skills for skiing downhill are grouped under Alpine skiing in Chapter 3; and skills enjoyable or useful whenever a skier becomes airborne are grouped under Ski Jumping in Chapter 4.

This is what it looks like in outline form:

Basic Skiing
— On-ski balance in walking-like strides
— On-ski balance when skis slide downhill
— On-ski balance when skis sideslip

Specialization
— Cross-country skiing
— Alpine skiing
— Ski jumping

In all four chapters, the focus is on fundamental **principles of motion**, not on polished styles. So the activities and practice exercises described **do not require special ski equipment.**

The approach for each maneuver is in two parts:
1) The maneuver, with an emphasis on its utility
2) The learning situation, involving:
   — The suitable terrain for learning
   — Practice exercises
   In Chapters 2 through 4, we also include:
   — Common learning problems and guidance examples

The first of these two parts concerns the underlying principles, which can be appreciated at any time, whenever you read this book. So we've put all explanations and peripheral details there.

■ But the second part, what you actually do out there on the snow, is far more brief and to the point, consisting of main headings and short verbal instructions you may use with a group. This useful brevity is emphasized by marking the text with a black box and making it stand out, like it does here.

The world of skiing is one of an infinite variety of terrains and snows, so there's no way we can tell you exactly how to instruct any given maneuver. Therefore, we've chosen typical instructional situations for all cases. After all, it's the skiing itself that teaches. So our method of instruction is one that gives activity high priority and exploits the situation at hand to benefit learning. We hope that this approach will aid you in prompting just that activity — skiing. After all, the best way to become a proficient skier is to ski a lot. No amount of formal instruction can take its place.

1 BASIC SKIING SKILLS

Let's say that you are a skiing parent or teacher, and a friend called you up on the phone and asked you: "I want to teach my kid to ski. How do I go about it? What should I do first, second, and so on?" You might be hard pressed for an answer, for there are many views on the subject.

Our cardinal rule for teaching kids to ski is to keep everything straightforward and simple, so we would answer any such question in a straightforward and simple manner.

First, we're dealing with children. So it helps to have some idea of how they learn. So we'll start by summarizing that topic as it applies to skiing — but only briefly, as so much has been written on it elsewhere. Second, we're dealing with skiing for children. So we've devoted the bulk of this book to **skiing** itself. Third and finally, skiing requires different gear and sometimes different clothing than used for other off-snow wintertime activities. As the joy of the sport is primary, we've put the discussion of gear last.

That's how we've organized this chapter on the basics.

HOW CHILDREN LEARN

Children must attain a certain level of maturity to be teachable. That's why formal schooling starts in most countries when children are six or seven years old.

Although these standards exist in most countries and seem to work well for schooling of large populations, little is known about the maturing process itself, or when abilities and potential should be stimulated.

One of the better measures of maturity is the average at which children show different interests and capabilities, both in mental abilities and motor skills. For instance, the set ages for first graders is based on the average child's ability to understand the information presented in school. They are old enough to be guided, or taught; they can understand what a teacher says and learn from it.

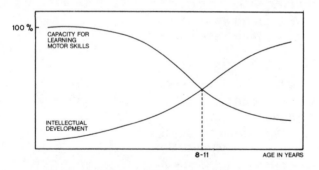

The capacity for learning motor skills is high at birth and diminishes thereafter. Up to age 4 or 5, motor skills develop characteristically as basic and gross movements, which are the foundations of future proficiencies. Ages 4 through 12 are especially important for learning new movement patterns and techniques. Proficiencies gained in this period are readily automated and well retained. Intellectual development makes children most receptive to schooling when they are 8 through 11 years old.

However, children are developed enough to learn skiing and other motor skills long before they have reached the stage of mental development necessary to handle school work. This may seem to be stating the obvious, as everyone knows that children learn to walk, run, jump, swim, ride bikes, and so on, long before they learn to count or read. Everyone knows that early childhood is the best time to learn those skills. But it's only been in the last couple of decades that the early stimulation of motor skills has been fully recognized.

Children have an enormous, spontaneous need to be active. Children are naturally energetic, and play involving physical skills can meaningfully use that energy. Motor skills are part of a child's total development, and frequently the most obvious part. A child's world is a physical world, one of constant, unbroken activity, eight hours or more a day. It's forced inactivity, not activity that exhausts small children. They are literally "built" for the former, and incapable of handling the latter.

However, there's probably only a handful of grade schools and kindergartens worldwide who are really aware of this aspect of child development. "Accepted fact" still seemingly dictates that late pre-school years and the first couple of years in school are the ideal times for teaching motor skills. Scientists in the field now regard those so-called **years of learning** as the **lost years**, because they are often too late to be efficient in achieving their purpose.

It's a real challenge to fully exploit the high receptiveness to motor learning in young children. That might be a reason for the delay to later years: the world of teaching (and theory of teaching) hasn't yet figured out how to instruct small children not yet mentally receptive to teaching according to its accepted, proven routines and methods. In other words, our fundamental guideline in teaching very young children to ski is **they're simply not teachable.** But before you give up, or toss this book out, we'll state our qualifier: Young children aren't teachable in the conventional sense of the word. The role of teacher or instructor is out of place. Instead, the role that teaches is that of arranger or organizer. In other words, if you pick the place and set the scene, children will learn, sometimes without further intervention on your part.

We cannot stress this aspect enough. So call this chapter "Creating situations in which children learn skiing naturally" if you will. There are plenty of parallels: If you are a parent, you undoubtedly remember that your children learned a lot about walking without your hovering over them all the time, instructing them in the art of that maneuver. It's the same way with skiing.

Rhythm first

Rhythm is as vital in skiing as it is in music. Without it, much is lost: Skiers, like musicians, can get off beat and ruin their performances. This doesn't mean that children must have musical talent to learn to ski well, but it does mean that the underlying rhythms of skiing maneuvers are more important than the technical perfections of their components. This is where many instructors err. "The knee should be here, not there; weight on this ski, not that one," and so on. Details like these are not vital. A child with good rhythm will pick up any needed fine points, but a child lacking rhythm in a maneuver still has much to learn, no matter how perfectly individual movements may be performed.

Just as in music, the essence of rhythm in skiing is to depart from regularity to avoid the monotony of repetition. Rhythm in skiing means that the right things happen at the right times. Exploiting the connection between the rhythm of a movement and the tonal image of a musical equivalent is a superb teaching aid. The syllables or words used may direct or command, as in many children's ditties. But their rhythmic content is more important. Single syllables, such as short words or even the tones of the diatonic scale can be chanted or sung. They don't even have to have any meaning. Words ending in vowels are particularly useful, as the vowel can be cut off or stretched out to suit the duration of the movement involved. Chanting "DO-DO!" "I SKIIII!" or similar simple combinations of words create clear audible images that do more to imbue rhythmic movement than any explanation of details.

The Learning Area

A "ski area" for children can be virtually any place there is snow. It's best to pick benign terrain not far from shelter and some plumbing, in case it's needed — which it usually is. A snow-covered school playground, golf course, pasture, or even a large back yard will do. Try to pick an area with a relatively large, flat surface with a gentle slope nearby; that will give you all you need to set the stage for learning basic skiing skills.

One word of caution should you pick plowed farmland for your "ski area": try to find an area where the ground surface was fairly even and level **and** well frozen before the snow fell. Furrows left by fall plowing can create unexpected obstacles just under the snow surface, and collect small pools of water, which when broken through to, can wet feet and legs quickly.

You'll be able to organize most of the basic skiing activities on this flat-plus-a-slope area. Most of the beginning on-ski maneuvers of this chapter are shown on the flat or on a slight slope. When kids are in the process of discovering skis and snow, they'll have enough to handle on this tame terrain.

But just as soon as they acquire some skiing skills, they will probably want to explore their new winter world. This doesn't mean that you must leave your tame terrain and seek another learning area. All you need to do is change the snow surface in a few places, and presto! — you have added a new dimension to the learning area. We have three favorite alterations: bicycle dips, roller-coaster dips, and bumps and jumps. Spades or car shovels are all you need to make them.

Bicycle dips are named for the up-down alternating leg motions necessary to ski through them. They teach balance, coordination, and independent arm and leg action on skis-plus they're a whale of a lot of fun. You can make them on the level or on a slight downhill; the slight downhill variety is shown in the drawing opposite. Pick a track where kids have skied with parallel skis, and alternately scoop out snow from one track to make a dip, and pile a bit of it up on the opposite track to make a hump. Finish by rounding off the dips and humps, and skiing through them. Space the crests of the humps about 12 feet apart, which is about right for real up-and-down leg action. Make the height difference between the bottoms of the dips and the crests of the humps no more than about half the leg length of the smallest child to ski through them.

If you're faced with loose snow that doesn't pack well, you can still make a set of gentle bicycle dips. First, make a set of tracks with a comfortable distance between your skis. Then ski the tracks, alternately forcefully down-weighting your skis: down hard for the dips, and up light for the humps. A spacing of about one and a half of your ski lengths between hump crests is about right.

Roller-coaster dips resemble bicycle dips, except that both tracks go up and down at the same places. They teach balance, coordination, and control of parallel skis. You can make them on a slight downhill. You can also make them on the flat, but as skiers only glide through them — they cannot "pump" for forward push as they can in bicycle dips — they have to be in a place where the skiers have some speed.

Jumps consist of a slope with a take-off ramp, followed by a safe sloped landing area. They make the skier airborne, which, aside from being a lot of fun, does wonders to overcome any fears of sliding speed and is great for building confidence in future Alpine skiers or ski jumpers.

By the numbers shown, the characteristics of a good, safe jump are:

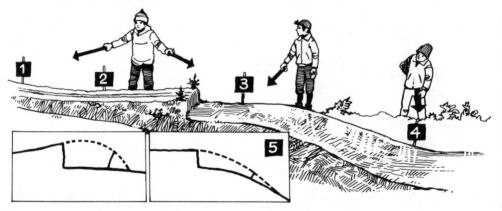

- Smooth, gentle transition from inrun slope to jump (1)
- Take-off area of jump should be level and about six to nine feet long (2)
- The landing slope should first be convex (3), then concave (4)
- The curves on the landing slope should be gentle, to ease balance upon landing and prevent injuries in falls
- Shape the takeoff area and the landing area slope so the landing angle is as small as possible (5)

- Good tracks to steer skis in the inrun before the takeoff
- A good place to start from
- Some marking of the edge, or "lip" of the jump. This is especially important on overcast days when there are no shadows to highlight features in the snow.
- A level, flat area following the jump outrun where skiers glide to a stop

With a little planning, you can shovel out a good jump and make other terrain variations at the same time. Here we've shown an example of a good jump on the left, followed left-to-right by a small "snow-bump," a downhill set of roller-coaster bumps, and a short slalom course.

How Balance Is Learned

The main goal of learning to ski at an early age is to promote balance, the ability to stand steadily on something in motion. For ordinary everyday situations children develop and their bodies automate the positional reflexes that counteract the pull of gravity on the various parts of the body. Skiing involves forces and movements that lie outside the sphere of this automated balance process.

Balance is largely controlled by sensory nerves in the soles of the feet. These sensors react to changes in pressure, and evoke reflexive muscular movements. In beginners, these reflexive movements may be extreme, as the "fine tuning," the smaller, deft movements in response to a stimulus are products of experience.

Maintaining balance while gliding at constant speed on an even underlying snow layer is only marginally more difficult than retaining balance while standing still. Apprehension and fear of speed, however, can disturb the process and upset balance, causing falls.

Skiing involves speed, which is one of the attributes contributing to the thrill of the sport.

Terrain slopes and snow surfaces vary. Speed increases and decreases continuously, and sometimes skiers become airborne and then land. The fine reflexes involved in balance must be trained to handle these situations. Balance is the very core of the ability to ski, which is why the three sections of this first part of the book are devoted to it: balance when striding, sliding downhill, and with skis sideslipping.

Balance isn't a maneuver which can be learned by being instructed or by copying others, as can, say, the various turns used in downhill skiing. Balance is the product of extensive and varied experience on skiis, an underlying fact which should be emphasized in all instructive situations. This also means that any specific style in skiing maneuvers isn't at all necessary or even desirable. What's important is the unconscious automating of the sensory detection-automatic reflex cycle.

A GOOD SEVEN

It's always difficult for adults to put themselves in children's shoes, which may be why the education of children is still a debated topic even after thousands of years of civilization. So it's always helpful to have a few reminders. Our favorite seven, each summarizing part of what we've said thus far, are:

- Children can learn to ski before they can comprehend what they are doing.
- Learning is more important than teaching.
- Rhythm is more important than technical finesse.
- Terrain teaches better than most people.
- Balance is vital; it's learned through lots of skiing.
- Ski gear does not produce skiing proficiency.
- Children are not small-sized adults; their skiing world is different.

STRIDE BALANCE

The quickest way to master the new and unfamiliar is to build on the old and familiar. This is why the various stride maneuvers on skis, movements closely resembling natural on-foot, off-snow motions, are the very foundation for starting children skiing. The end product of highly-developed stride techniques is, of course, cross-country skiing. But for the purposes of learning the basics and imbuing balance, on-ski strides are the most direct link to what most children can already do. For kids, the various elementary ski strides and maneuvers also provide on-snow freedom, a freedom to go where their interest takes them. These are the reasons we put strides first in the entire learning sequence.

There are many ways to "walk on skis," with skis:

- **Parallel,** as in the diagonal stride, traversing, and side-stepping.
- **With tips spread and tails together,** as in herringboning and skating.
- **Alternating between parallel and angled positions,** as in skate turns.

We'll talk about each of these basic maneuvers in turn.

Skiing starts as simple walking on snow, with no glide. Here a two-year-old takes the first few shaky ski steps, gingerly striding only half a small foot's length at a time. The first reactions to skis can be mixed, but tots usually rapidly forget the strange objects on their feet and adapt quickly to them.

Here's a slightly older child who has learned some balance skills and is trying to stride out on skis — but on-ski balance is not yet good enough for an efficient **kick,** or walk-like push-off on the propelling foot. Note: the child typically seeks security against forward falls by carrying the ski poles forward, ahead of the body. So it really doesn't matter if poles are short, as they are used mostly for stability.

Opinions vary as to whether or not children should use ski poles when first learning to ski. Aside from the safety aspects, which we discuss later in the equipment section, we're not strongly convinced one way or the other. Our advice is that if a child wants to use poles, let him/her have them. Poles are a part of skiing, and they are often an aid to balance for beginning skiers. But many children also like to start skiing without poles. If this is the case, let them; the challenge to balance is greater without poles, so they may learn balance more quickly.

Poles or no poles is the question. Here a child wonders what to do with the strange sticks with loops — what are they for?

Glide Stride

Children soon discover that they may be able to ski faster than they can walk. And they soon find that the way to get that speed is to push-off, or **kick** harder with each stride, much as they would do to go from a walk to a jog on foot. But as soon as they kick harder, they meet new balance problems, because their skis glide more. This is one of the first stages when ski proficiency becomes enjoyable for children. It's exciting to learn the art of not falling as speed increases and decreases with each kicking step. They set their own challenge by striding as best they can.

This five-year-old girl skis well with diagonal rhythm, with opposite arm and leg moving in unison. She has a good stride and gets good glide with each kick. She glides on both skis in the stride position; this is what we call the **glide stride.**

As balance improves, body weight comes more forward, over the leading ski. This improves ski grip during kicks and makes it easier to maintain a good rhythm without tiring.

Adults, as well as children, use the glide stride to save effort in touring. This is why it's sometimes called the **touring stride.** It's a stable and relaxing way to tour ski at a leisurely speed.

Although the glide stride is itself a useful maneuver on skis, it is also an intermediate phase of learning the more efficient **diagonal stride.** The diagonal stride is to the glide stride what jogging is to walking. The desire to ski faster is the impetus that develops the diagonal stride, the most-used stride in cross-country skiing.

The glide stride is frequently used by recreational touring skiers.

KICK   GLIDE   KICK

Here's a girl enjoying the thrill of self-propelled skiing speed. Her upper body is well forward, her hips are angled well for an efficient kick, and her coordination and rhythm are good. Her kicks aren't short and rapid, but rather slower and more drawn out, and she glides on both skis, as in the glide stride. But her speed, good crouch when kicks start, and weight well forward set her skiing apart from the simpler glide stride. She is on her way to learning a good diagonal stride. We'll say more about the diagonal stride in Chapter 2.

Uphill strides

Skis slip easily on uphills, so special strides are used to go uphill: traversing, sidestep, and herringbone. The basic difference between these maneuvers and the glide stride is that the skis are **edged.** Edging skis helps children build ankle strength and stability that will be useful later in executing turns on skis.

Side stepping is most useful on steeper slopes, but can be learned on a gradual slope where it's easier to edge skis into the hill. It can be learned as shown here, just by walking sideways up the slope.

Sidestep

Traversing is a combination of side stepping and the glide stride. It is most used on long, moderate slopes. The upper ski is lifted up and forward at an angle to the slope, and the lower ski follows.

Herringbone, named for the pattern the skis leave in the snow, is most used on slopes where a direct uphill glide stride slips backwards. Ski tips are spread into a V, and the skier walks uphill in a duck waddle. The steeper the hill, the wider the V.

Traversing

Skating and Skate Turning

With better balance and stronger, more stable ankle control giving edging ability, children can rapidly develop technique and learn other maneuvers. Skating and skate turning are valuable and thoroughly enjoyable maneuvers to use at this stage. They also lend themselves well to use in group classes, even if confined to a small area. These maneuvers allow many variations, don't require any special ski waxing, and result in skills useful in all other forms of skiing.

Herringbone

Skating on skis is like skating on roller or ice skates: movements are forward, with alternate outward angling of skis. The forward power comes from kicking from one ski and gliding on the other.

Skate turning differs from pure skating in that pushes come only from the outer ski in a turn. So the strides alternate between parallel skis and spread skis.

Skating and stake turning are amazingly universal and extremely rapid learning exercises because:

- Children clearly feel how to shift weight from one ski to the other.
- The maneuvers require gliding on one ski, which is balance practice of value for cross-country technique.
- Both skating and skate turning are exercises for strength and moving stability in leg muscles as well as in ankles.

The Learning Situation

Acquiring balance on skis takes time. Children pick it up more quickly than do adults, but they are usually less motivated for skiing itself and may lose interest quickly. Children simply are not small-scale adults.

Adult recreations, such as tours, are often tiring for children, whether or not they are on skis. Their attention spans are simply too short for them to enjoy doing the same thing for any length of time. So introducing children to skiing skills often requires a special approach keyed to their needs and capabilities through suitably arranged learning situations. One of the best ways to introduce children to skiing skills is through games. Almost any game that can be played on foot can be played on skis.

TERRAIN

Children are naturally curious; there's seldom any need to motivate their desire to explore and investigate. This is why the terrain variations in a learning ski area are themselves aids to maintaining pupil interest. But as the ideal learning area is flat with only a few gentle slopes around, sometimes excitement has to be made if it's not there naturally. Here are a few of our favorite, special on-ski situations high in learning value:

- **Trackland** is an on-snow variety of a paper chase. Tracks of varying lengths, with turns and crossings, are laid out and marked, usually with crepe paper streamers. Skiers can follow a certain color—"ski the red track," count how many streamers marked the track, or look for other signs erected along the way.

- **Snow Wonderland:** Snow on trees and branches tempts the imagination to see a variety of forms. A few additions—twigs, pine cones, a ski pole—can enhance the scene with real and mythical people and animals. Here a tour is really one into the fantasy of winter.

- **Snow Storyland.** It's always easy to base games on well-known children's stories, because everyone knows what to do. Stories involving chases are particularly easy to arrange, especially if you have new snow on hand. For instance, the "cowboys" (on skis) follow the "tracks" of "Indians" (also on skis) or vice versa. There can be "rewards" for finding the quarry. For adults, following a ski track made by another skier may seem outlandishly obvious—but for children that's just the point.

- **Ski Traffic Wise.** Set up a few "traffic signs" along a short trail, preferably of the European pictorial type now coming into use in the U.S. Lay out the trail accordingly, with bumps, turns, intersections and the like. Children ski the track, obeying the signs. Children can ski together to play the part of larger vehicles: two children holding hands are a van, three together towing each other with poles are a truck or bus, and so on.

PRACTICE

■ **SMALLEST, LONGEST, FASTEST**
Who can ski with the shortest, longest, fastest strides?

■ **DECORATION**
Move ski tips and/or tails; make varied flower and leaf patterns in the snow.

■ **SCOOTER**
Skiers on one ski only, in a straight, stable track, kicking scooter-like with the other foot. A pole can be held crosswise to simulate "handlebars." The goal is to glide with even, steady kicks. Change skis and repeat game.

Note:
- Good stance (2, 3)
- Full extension (3)
- Good weight transfer, good balance (4, 5)
- Sinking crouch before next kick (5, 6)

KICK **GLIDE**

■ **SIDECAR**
A two-skier version of the SCOOTER, done side-by-side, arms around each other's shoulders for stability, skis on outer feet, inner feet for kicking.
- Who can glide the farthest on each kick?
- Who can ski the fastest?

■ **SKATER**
Who's the fastest speed skater?

With good snow conditions and skis that grip and glide well, SIDECAR can be played with both skiers wearing two skis. One variation of the four-ski sidecar is for both skiers to kick a couple of times, alternately left, then right, with even rhythm.

■ RELAYS
Teams divide up on either end of a straight stretch, 100 to 200 feet long, and skiers skate in between tags.

■ FLAT SLALOM
Lay out a zig-zag course on the flat, with poles or other markers at the turns. The skiers skate the course; after a while they will skate turn around the poles. This can be arranged as a relay, but then preferably without poles.

■ FIGURE EIGHTS
Lay out two adjacent circles, each about 12 to 18 feet in diameter and about six feet apart, marking them off with poles or other markers. Two skiers skate a figure eight around the course. Match the diameters of the circles to the skiers' skating proficiencies.

How to Fall Without Hurting Yourself, How to Get Up

Falls are unavoidable, and if not done properly, they can both hurt and frighten. So falls should be a natural part of early learning.

For instance, there are several hazards in forward falls: hitting the chest so hard as to knock breath out, abrading the face, or hitting the nose so hard as to cause nose bleeding. Danger also lurks in sideways falls. Often skiers, especially children, fall sideways with a knee hitting the snow first. Heavy snow and a little speed are all that's necessary to turn a knee-first sideways fall into one that injures through twisting.

Chance of injury and fear of falling are lessened if children have experience in falling. Repeated, intentional falls teach children how to hit the snow, and where they should be stiff and where they should be loose. Start fall practice in a standstill, squatting position. In addition to learning to hit the snow, it's important to practice:

- Falling to the side.
- Falling so the buttocks hit the snow first.
- Straightening out trunk and legs when down.
- Preventing body from rotating about skis.
- Lying still until motion has stopped.

Initial practice should be at a standstill. But once it's mastered, add a bit of speed, and you'll see that kids find falling fun.

How to get up. First, skis up to untangle them, to make it easier to get up. For falls on hills, set skis on downhill side of the body before getting up.

DOWNHILL BALANCE

We say that skis, like sled runners, **glide** when they slide forward in the direction the ski is pointed, as opposed to **slip** when skis unintentionally slide backwards, or slide to the side. Gliding is part of skiing down a slope, through bicycle or roller-coaster dips, when jumping, or when changing direction with step or skate turns.

It's exciting for children to balance on gliding skis, so there's seldom any problem in getting them to practice it. Glide practice builds ability to control skis and body, and improves balance. In the process, children usually discover how the shape and springiness of skis can be used to steer the skis.

I watch where I'm going so I can ski straight.

A. Position of readiness
- Weight equally on both skis
- Entire foot weighted
- Relaxed shoulders
- Slight bend at hips, knees and ankles

B. Terrain contact
- "Rubber" knees
- Good contact between skis and snow
- Knees and body "absorb" a bump

Many children glide on skis early while they are developing balance. Sometimes they need help, both for support on downhills and for motive power back uphill, as shown in these two drawings of adults assisting a two-year-old girl. If longer assist poles are used, several kids can be supported or towed at the same time.

Children can learn to brake speed or stop after a downhill slide by a step turn or a skating turn on the following flat. This enables them to ski steeper hills.

The step turn, as its name implies, is simply a successive, alternate stepping of the skis in a new direction. Tips are alternately spread and brought together until the skis are pointed in the new direction.

The Learning Situation

TERRAIN

The first glides should be on a gentle slope, only a few yards long, where the children either start at the top or from a small plateau on the hill, and can glide to a stop on a flat below the slope.

Excitement is a major motivation in child's play. If children master one situation, it can become unexciting, and they will seek another; they tire quickly of repetition. You can meet the need for varied and increasing challenge simply by the way you arrange activities. For instance, the challenge of a single downhill slope can be varied through:

- Finding parts of it of different length or inclination.
- Letting children glide downhill in good tracks or in loose snow.
- Finding or making variations in the snow surface in or alongside the track.
- Changing direction during a downhill glide.

It's not enough to make just one track with bicycle dips, one with roller-coaster dips, and so forth; you have to make several. Vary track profiles through these areas to suit different speeds, different heights of bumps and depths of dips, and so on. Small jumps and snow bumps also test balance, and can be made to provide a range of challenges.

PRACTICE

There must be an infinite number of games to teach balance on downhill glides. Here are ten of our favorites:

- **COCK-A-DOODLE-DO!**
  Ski downhill without poles, flap your wings like a rooster, and then lift one leg and crow "COCK-A-DOODLE-DO!" After a couple of tries, the skiers will probably be so brave that they'll flap, hop and crow at the same time.

■ **GRAB SNOW**

Ski downhill without poles, and bend at the knees to pick up snow, alternately with left and right hands. Who can pick up enough on the downhill run to make a snowball and throw it at you?

■ **PICK-UP**

Like GRAB SNOW, but skiers pick up objects like pieces of cloth, twigs, and the like. If it's a warm day and some kids have shucked their caps, gloves, or mittens, you can use these as pick-ups (but be sure they don't get too wet if the kids have to wear them home).

■ **JUGGLER**

Ski downhill balancing a snowball on the head. Who can ski the farthest without losing the snowball?

■ **WINDY DAY**

Who can ski downhill and wiggle like a tall tree blown by the wind?

■ **CHUG-CHUG!**

Pretend you're a little steam engine, chugging downhill, shifting to the left and the right over imaginary switches in the track. If this works well, have the skiers jump up slightly at each "switch" with an up-down or down-up rhythm.

■ **UP-DOWN**

Set up two or more "arches" on a downhill track by planting poles on either side of the track and suspending a horizontal pole between the wrist loops (on the downhill side of the vertical poles, for safety's sake). Just after each "arch" suspend a cloth or paper streamer from a branch or pole stuck in the snow, at about head height. The skiers ski downhill, bending at the knees to go through the "arches," and rising up to touch the streamers.

- Move the streamers closer to the "arches" for faster reactions.
- Set "arches" and streamers at differing distances from each other, so the skiers must vary rhythms, sharpening their reactions.

■ YO-YO
What goes down must come up: after a short downhill run, have the skiers step turn to the left on the flat below. If all goes well, have them skate harder to the left, until they have turned around and are headed back uphill. Then reverse directions, with skates to the right.

■ SLALOM
Set up a zig-zag slalom course with poles or other markers. Two poles indicate a complete turn to the opposite direction. Put a few up-down "arches" in the course. Fasten a streamer to a pole or branch to one side of the last pole or "arch" and have the skiers ski over and touch it to "finish." This will prevent a traffic jam at the last pole.

■ PATHFINDER
Set up a maze of poles and markers on the slope, and let the skiers find their own ways downhill by changing direction, skating, and turning, all without stopping. Skiing in pairs through the maze makes it more exciting.

Terrain Teaches
ROLLER-COASTER DIPS

Here's an easy roller-coaster, with small humps for low speed. The four-year-old boy skiing here balances well, but sits a bit low on his skis. The effect is for the first hump (1, 2, 3) to knock him upwards, pushing his upper body up from his skis (4, 5). He then resumes his low squat (6), which again results in an upward jolt (7, 8).

Here's the same boy a few days later. The jolts of his first experience with the roller-coaster have taught him to dampen the bumps by standing a bit more erect in the dips (2). He "absorbs" a bump by letting it push his knees up towards his chest, while his upper body remains fairly stable (3, 4). The terrain has been his teacher; he now has greater control of his skiing.

TRANSITION TO A FLAT

Flats, changing to slopes, and back to flats again are part of typical ski terrain. Here's how a five-year-old boy skied this type of terrain on his first try, and after a bit of practice.

FIRST TRY

WITH PRACTICE

On his first try, he fell on the transition to the flat. But after a bit of practice he mastered the terrain variations and was steady on his skis, even if he started fast at the top of the hill.

BICYCLE DIPS

Here's a typical set of downhill bicycle dips, with a relatively large vertical spacing between dip bottom and bump crest.

Here a five-year-old meets the challenge of the hill. He skis fast into the bicycle dips, and his legs pump him through, giving him good practice in individual leg work. Note that he plays it safe by leaning back on his skis.

JUMPS

Young children believe in their hearts that they can fly, because they have flown in their dreams. On skis they have a good chance to realize their dreams, so they'll usually want to jump before they have acquired the balance necessary for the maneuver. In trying, they learn to fall and get up, learn to tolerate a tumble, and learn the limits of their balance abilities. Here's a typical scene on a first try:

First try.

Here a good, solid inrun and a real leap into the air result in a hard fall and a sore behind.

With some practice.

But with a bit of experience, the skier stands on every jump. Again, the terrain has taught. But we also see that the skier is less ambitious on the takeoff.

SIDESLIP BALANCE

We say that skis **sideslip** when they slide on the snow directly or at an angle to the side. Sideslips occur in two general ways:

- With skis in a plow position and in a plow turn.
- With skis parallel, as in downhill ski turns.

In this chapter we'll discuss the elementary plow forms. The more advanced parallel-ski sideslipping is part of Alpine skiing technique, covered in Chapter 3.

Sideslipping allows speed to be controlled. The more skis sideslip and the more they are edged, the more they slow speed.

There are a few obvious and a few more subtle reasons for teaching these braking maneuvers:

- Ability to control speed on downhills promotes a feeling of security.
- Safety is increased when skiers can control speed to avoid collisions.
- The experience and feeling of a sideslipping ski's movement and control in snow gives confidence.
- The maneuvers build balance, strength and stability in the ankles, and therefore aid future learning of turns.

In the downhill snowplow, both skis sideslip, or "plow up" snow, with tips together and tails spread. The sideslipping is symmetrical, on the inner edges of the skis: the right edge of the left ski and the left edge of the right ski.

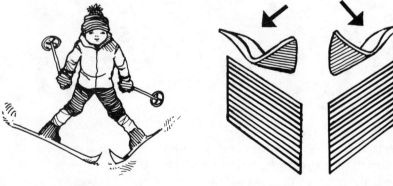

Snowplow.   *Sideslip in plow position.*

As soon as children feel secure in snow-plowing and controlling their sideslipping skis, they will start turning—often without anyone telling them to do so.

FALL-LINE

The snowplow turn is a turn over the fall-line of the slope with the skis in a plow position. A turn is initiated by increasing weight on one ski. For instance, to start a turn to the left, the left ski tip can be lifted a bit. The left ski then brakes less, and the right ski, pointed to the left, initiates the turn.

For many children, the plow turn is just a step on the way to learning parallel turns. But as any ski mountaineer or wilderness skier can attest, the snowplow turn is very useful in tough terrain, especially when carrying a heavy pack. It's a turn that all should know.

The Learning Situation

TERRAIN

Turns are best taught on a well-packed, slight downhill slope that ends in a well-packed flat. A slightly bowed hill, convex across the fall-line, is best, because it will be easy to hold a plow position with outer edges clear of the snow. As they gain skill, children can practice snowplowing on steeper, less regular slopes.

PRACTICE

■ THE SLIDE

Mark off a broad chute straight down the slope, using poles or branches, and tell the skiers they can play many of the games on it that they play on playground slides. First, have them all plow down the chute to make a smooth surface. Then play games:

- Snowplow slowly straight downhill, ski tips together, tails wide apart.
- Snowplow downhill in pairs, side-by-side, with a narrower, faster plow.
- Ski straight downhill, plowing with one ski. Change plowed ski on next run.
- Ski straight down into chute and stop with a plow. Who stops fastest?
- "Car and trailer" one after the other, plowing and holding poles.
- Same as "car and trailer," but with the first skier braking, the other gliding.

■ BUNNY

Pretend that you're rabbits, hopping downhill as you flow down the fall-line. On the first few runs, have the skiers just bend in the knees, as if preparing to hop. When they get the hang of the bend, tell them to hop, like bunnies.

■ THE LANDING
Pretend that you're airplanes, landing on the downhill slope. Ski downhill without poles, arms outstretched like airplane wings.
- Land with shortest possible stopping distance.
- Approach faster and brake to a stop.
- Fast approach, brake, new start to "taxi," and then brake to a stop.

■ FAST-SLOW
Set alternating narrow and wide gates, each marked by poles on either side of the fall-line.
- Ski straight down through the narrow gates, and plow through the wide gates.
- Ski in pairs, one after the other, with second skier trying to keep a fixed distance from the first.

Two sets of fast-slow gates parallel to each other allow the skiers to ski side-by-side, with one being the pace setter and the other following.

■ ZIG-ZAG
Mark off a corridor, nine to ten feet wide, with poles spaced ten to twelve feet apart. Mark the poles on either side with different colored streamers, such as red on the right and blue on the left. Give each skier a bit of streamer to hold in each hand, red in the right, blue in the left.

- In a snowplow without ski poles, ski downhill, touching "red" poles with "red" hands and "blue" poles with "blue" hands.
- Repeat, but with a little more speed skiing into the corridor.

Lengthen and widen the corridor for longer turns.

■ THE HALL

This is an on-snow equivalent of the natural temptation for children to run not straight, but zig-zag down halls, touching the walls. Mark off a downhill corridor about six feet wide.

The skiers plow down the corridor, alternately pushing right and left ski tails towards the poles marking the "walls."

- Repeat, but at greater speed, with more knee bend.
- Repeat, but try to tap each "wall" pole with the tips of the fingers of an outstretched arm. Here the poles may be marked as in ZIG-ZAG.

Widening and lengthening the corridor will teach the children controlled plow turns.

■ THE SNAKE

Set up zig-zag line of poles down the hill, about 12 to 15 feet apart, alternating placing a foot and a half or two on either side of the fall-line. Tell the skiers that they must ski down, around the outside of each pole, wiggling like a snake.

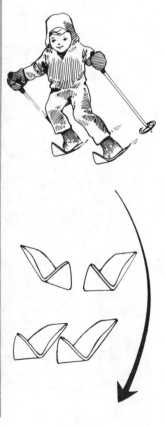

- Ski downhill, through the "wiggle."
- Repeat, in more of a crouch, with greater knee bend.
- Repeat, but get up a little speed before skiing into the "wiggle."

Here's where you'll see the greatest differences among young skiers. Some feel comfortable with a broad snowplow, while others get along with a narrower vee of their skis. Some children will flatten or even reverse edges on the inside ski or a turn as they ski fast. Resist the temptation to correct these children. Remember, the final goal is to ski with skis parallel (Chapter 3).

IT'S A NATURAL

One of the joys of skiing is using it to do something else.

Skiing is much more than just a recreational activity, which is perhaps the key to the sport's many joys. "Those who ski," French author Jean-Paul Sartre once remarked, "have a most enjoyable game to play."

And a game it should always be, especially for those who are learning the skills that will serve them through a lifetime of enjoying the sport. So as soon as children can move and balance, glide on skis and control their speed, you should introduce them to the world of winter. Take them on a short tour. It can be just around the frozen tees of a snow-covered golf course or through a small grove of trees, but maybe on the way you'll see something new — a bird track in the snow, a strangely-formed icicle hanging from a branch. Skiing is so much more than just games and drills on your teaching hill and flat.

EQUIPMENT PRIMER

Just as in skiing itself, in equipment, the simple approach is best. We believe there is only one rule in selecting ski equipment for children learning to ski:

> **Ski equipment should always aid, and never detract from their learning of skiing.**

Though simple, this rule is sometimes difficult to practice. Some ski shops have a bewildering array of gear for kids; others have little or nothing. Some parents or teachers, especially those who have recently purchased kid's gear themselves, often have strong opinions on it. What you see other kids using isn't always a good guide; after all, they didn't have much say in the selection.

So before we discuss the details of any equipment item — and that discussion will be brief because we rank skiing far above its paraphernalia — we'll let you in on a fairly obvious secret: there are four general guidelines for selecting children's gear.

How do you outfit a child for skiing? Here's a preschooler sporting utilitarian gear.

1 Keep it simple and basic. Just as children learn to walk before they run and ride tricycles before they ride bicycles, they start skiing with the rudimentary basics. For them, skis are initially just cumbersome shoes. Think of that when viewing gear; consider the tricycles of skiing, and leave the top-end stuff to later, much later.

2 Gear may change by the year but kids don't. The latest "wonders" are seldom best for kids. A two-year-old learning to ski in the

1980's goes through the same processes and makes the same mistakes as did the two-year-olds of the last generation — or, for that matter, the last five or ten generations. If you've ever seen century-old children's skis in a ski museum you've probably thought them to be pretty advanced for their time. Snow hasn't changed and neither have the kids. . .

3 **When in doubt, ski and see.** If you doubt the utility of any item of gear, postpone purchase. Instead, rent, borrow, trade at ski swaps or whatever. Kids will wear out gear fast enough as it is. Experiment a bit. Kids may think it's great to try different stuff. And besides, they'll probably let you know when something suitable comes along.

4 **Style is usually useless.** Let's face it: tots on skis, the pre-schoolers of this Chapter, spend almost as much time in the snow as they do on top of it. They get tangled up. They get snow all over themselves. They are hard on their gear. So in selecting anything for their skiing use, think of the punishment it's going to get — and the work parents will have in maintaining it if it doesn't hold up to that punishment.

These four guidelines don't say that kids will or should look like ragamuffins on skis. What they do say is that utility should be your only goal in selecting gear; all other facets are secondary. If you cannot understand the utility of a particular feature of an item, you're probably better off forgetting that item. Having said that, we'll now talk a bit about the features of the various items.

Skis

Broad, sturdy cross-country-type skis fitted with simple toepiece bindings that hold the heel with a strap or cable, and flexible boots are by the far the best choices for children learning to ski.

Two general types of skis for small children are available: **junior skis** and **children's skis**. Types and designations are often mixed, so we will define them in their strict sense, as shown in the drawing. **Junior skis** are scaled-down versions of adult models, primarily intended for eight- to fourteen-year-olds. **Children's skis** are designed for tots through first-graders, as much for on-snow play as for the various technical skiing maneuvers. Junior skis are sometimes thinner, but otherwise look like adult skis, while children's skis are broader in relation to their length and are designed to hold simple strap or toepiece bindings. They are made to be inexpensive, and therefore have a simpler construction than do junior skis or adult skis.

Skis should be relatively short, seldom more than head height. Skis for young tots, two or three years old, can even be shorter than head height. For initial on-snow play and games, the shorter the ski the better. It's better for children to outgrow skis than to be expected to grow into them. It's only later, as they stride better and ski faster, that they need extra length.

All skis have camber, the bow of the center of the ski up above its tip and tail, and stiff-

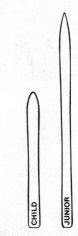

Children's skis are designed for tots; junior skis are scaled-down versions of adult skis.

CHILD   JUNIOR

Children use shorter skis in relation to their body height than do teenagers or adults.

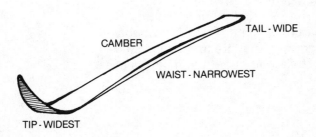

TAIL - WIDE

CAMBER

WAIST - NARROWEST

TIP - WIDEST

ness, the resistance to flattening that bow. The major problem in selecting cambers and stiffnesses in children's skis is to find pairs where they are small enough, not large enough. In general, skis for tots should be so soft that when placed base-to-base, an adult parent can squeeze their bases flat using the thumb and forefingers of one hand only. Skis with little camber or rounded edges are often preferable, as they are easier to turn on snow.

Children's skis should have a pronounced sidecut. That is, when viewed from above, they should have an hourglass shape, with waist narrower than tip and tail. Skis with sidecuts track well in snow and are easier for kids to control than skis with straighter sides.

In the last couple of decades, one of the few real improvements in children's skis has been in their bases. Drawing on developments in cross-country ski bases, good wax-holding plastic bases and plastic waxless bases are now available. If you are a cross-country skier who prefers waxable skis and don't mind waxing your children's skis, then select waxable skis for them, by all means. But otherwise we recommend the waxless variety, as they relieve you of the chore of waxing. Pattern-type waxless bases are best, as they are sturdier and less likely to pick up dirt than are the hair-type bases.

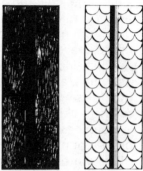

WAXABLE   WAXLESS

A waxable ski base (left) is smooth; a pattern-type waxless base (right) has irregularities that dig into the snow for grip.

Boots

Boots for small children should be waterproof, fit well, be large enough so they may be worn with two or more pairs of socks for warmth, and be stable on the foot. Best are over-ankle boots that are high enough to give support, and are fitted with a snow cuff that at least keeps most of the snow out of the boot in falls and play in the snow. Tots can use standard children's galoshes, which fit the simple strap

A good boot supports the ankle.

bindings of the smaller children's skis. Some models of ordinary children's outdoor boots can fit into adjustable ski bindings, and work well. Older children, five and six year-olds, can use 71 millimeter toe width Nordic Norm cross-country ski boots. Most models of these boots have sturdy rubber soles that are flexible enough for walking and other off-ski activities, and pile lining for warmth. Kids can put these boots on in the morning and be ready to ski later in the day. All of these boots — galoshes, hiking boots, and Nordic Norm cross-country ski boots — can be used for other wintertime activities, which is an advantage, because boots are usually rapidly outgrown.

Bindings

Bindings should be:
— Simple, so children can learn to operate them.
— Designed for maximum forward foot flex, for ease of striding.
— Sideways stable, so they hold a weighted foot on a ski.
— Good mates to the boots with which they are used.

Three types of children's bindings satisfy these utilitarian requirements: simple strap bindings, toe bindings, and heel strap/cable bindings.

Strap bindings are the simplest available, and consist of a simple strap or a strap and a leather or fabric cup to hold ordinary galoshes. They allow full forward foot freedom. However, they offer little sideways stability, and permit boot toes to slide a bit on the ski. These are minor drawbacks considering the utility of this type for the smallest children. We recommend them for two- and three-year-olds.

Toe bindings for children resemble cross-country ski bindings for adults. They allow good forward foot freedom and good sideways stability, basically because the binding ears extend back about a third of the length of the boot sole welt. Children sometimes have difficulty learning to use toe bindings, as they have to learn to push their boot far enough into the binding to allow the bail to be depressed to hold the boot. But this is a minor drawback: the old reliable 71-mm Nordic Norm pin binding has been around for a long time — it's proven dependable and almost completely child-proof.

Heel strap/cable bindings resemble toe bindings with a strap/cable attached. We recommend them as all-round children's bindings: they allow good forward foot freedom and excellent sideways stability. They restrict forward flex a bit more than do toe bindings, because the heel strap/cable pressure increases as the foot is flexed forward. However, they are easy to understand and operate, and most children can quickly learn to operate them without assistance.

Poles

Select poles long enough to reach up to a child's armpit, but no more. It doesn't matter if they are shorter or the child grows a bit during the season. Shorter poles are easier to handle. A child's first pair of poles should **not** have metal tips, as do adult and junior poles. They should rather be fitted with **safety tips**, rounded plastic or hard rubber ends that cannot injure as metal tips can. Wrist straps need not be adjustable, but they should be of leather or synthetic leather, and not a plastic that will stiffen and chafe in the cold.

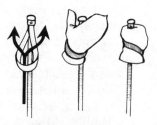

How to hold a pole.

Clothing

There are probably as many ways to clothe children for outdoor activity as there are parents who clothe those children. So we'll only mention a few guidelines:

- Don't bundle kids up like Eskimos; it restricts their movement on skis.
- But remember that children do feel colder than adults at the same temperature. Many light layers is the best approach.
- Wool is fine, but not as an outer garment: it picks up snow and absorbs water.
- Waterproof outer layers are best; remember how often kids are down in the snow.
- Spare caps and mittens or gloves are a must. You'll be amazed how quickly these items can be lost, even in so small a place as the back seat of a car.
- Avoid scarves if possible; they tend to work loose and get tangled in things children come in contact with, posing a hazard.
- Pick outer clothing with large zippers or buttons that the children themselves can learn to operate with cold fingers.
- Favor garments that you can wash or clean at home. You'll be amazed how much dirt kids can sometimes pick up from a seemingly pristine field of snow.

Waxing

In the basic skiing of this chapter, children move on skis on the flat, uphill, and downhill. For them, the world of skiing is like skiing once was in its entirety: a utilitarian mode of over-snow transport. Today this all-terrain approach, the modern version of traditional skiing, goes by the name of cross-country.

So the waxes needed for waxable children's skis are cross-country ski waxes. Their action is simple. When a ski is correctly waxed, the microscopic irregularities in the underlying snow surface penetrate the wax just enough so a motionless ski has bite, or "grip" on the snow. But when a ski is in motion over the same snow surface, the irregularities do not dig into the wax. In fact, they even melt slightly so the ski glides on a microscopic water layer. The better the waxing, the greater the difference between ski grip and ski glide.

There are many options in cross-country waxing, ranging from simple two-wax systems up to complete ranges of products to fine tune skis to snow. We believe that the two-wax systems are the best for most recreational skiers and great for kids. Two waxes, a cork and a scraper aren't much to keep track of, and older children can easily learn to wax their own skis without adult assistance. It's part of their enjoyment of the sport. Don't confuse them with complete arrays, as used by racers. Leave that until later, if they decide they want to go in for cross-country ski racing.

The waxes of the two-wax systems are brewed to work on broad ranges of snow conditions, one type for temperatures below freezing and one type for temperatures above freezing. Some cross-country purists scoff at this simple approach. But their disdain is unjustified, as two-wax systems have been used on major ski expeditions, and even top international racers occasionally use them for tricky conditions. In short, they're simple and they work well. Follow the manufacturer's directions, and you'll seldom go wrong.

Our advice on brands is to select one that is available where you live or where you ski, and learn to use it well. The four most commonly available brands are listed in the table below:

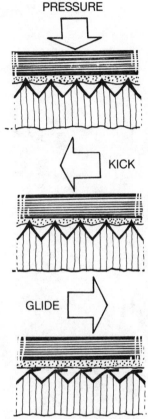

Microscopic irregularities in snow dig into a motionless, weighted ski, so you can kick forward, but don't dig into wax of a gliding ski.

TWO-WAX SYSTEMS

Temperature		Snow	Apply Wax	Brands			
°F	°C			Jack Rabbit	Rex Universal	Swix Two-wax	Toko Touring
above	+	Slop	Rough	WET	PLUS	SILVER	PLUS
		Wet	Smooth				
32°	0°	Dry	Rough	DRY	MINUS	GOLD	MINUS
below	–	Powder	Smooth				

(Table by permission, from *Waxing for Cross-Country Skiing*, by M. Brady and L. Skjemstad, Wilderness Press, Berkeley, 6th edition, 1981)

A wilderness downhill run.

2 CROSS-COUNTRY

Cross-country skiing is a continuation of all the basic skiing skills covered in Chapter 1, with the emphasis on efficient ski techniques to cover distance in terrain.

Cross-country skiing is actually the least specialized form of skiing, which is perhaps one of the major factors in the fairly recent worldwide renaissance of the sport. This is why we always recommend cross-country to children (or their parents) who are undecided as to what form of skiing they should pursue once they have mastered basic skiing skills. Cross-country is always an excellent foundation for all types of skiing because:

- It uses all possible ski characteristics such as glide, grip, and camber.
- It builds all-around balance and feeling for terrain.
- It involves rhythmic exercise without excess muscular stress of any muscle group.
- It is effective self-propelled motion through alternating effort and relaxation.

A WORD ON GEAR

Up until a few years ago, junior models of special cross-country touring, light touring, and racing skis were unavailable outside of Scandinavia. Now, thanks to the burgeoning numbers of cross-country skiers worldwide, they are available almost everywhere cross-country skiing is done. For children still learning skiing basics and taking up cross-country, we recommend the sturdier touring category of gear: broader skis, higher boots, and stronger bindings. This is the kind of gear used by the kids shown in the illustrations of this chapter. It's not only good enough for learning superb cross-country ski technique, but it will take an incredible amount of punishment in the process. So much information is now available on cross-country gear — in shops and cross-country ski areas, and in books and magazines (we list some good references in the back of this book) — that we won't say any more about it in this book.

THE CROSS-COUNTRY LEARNING AREA

If you can teach cross-country skills at a cross-country ski area and can use their shorter trails, all the better. If not, don't despair, but lay out a few shorter trails of your own, building in your own terrain variations if necessary — roller-coaster dips, bicycle dips, sharp skating turns, zig-zag trails and the like.

In fact, you don't need very much area to lay out a top-notch cross-country learning area; a few acres will do. Start with a flat area for basic instruction, and ski out one or more trails in the nearby terrain, as shown here.

Make the trails in loops, and mark the length of each at its start. It's a good idea to state trail length in meters or kilometers, now used for all cross-country trails throughout the world, including the U.S. and Canada. We've illustrated here with three trails, varying from 200 meters to 600 meters in length (a meter is about ten percent longer than a yard). If you set trails that will remain undisturbed for several learning sessions, you might find signs a useful aid. Place pictorial instructive signs along the way, telling the skiers what maneuvers are best at those points. A play-oriented variation of the sign-posted track is one with small mini-playgrounds along the way, each with a task, such as throwing balls against targets.

Ski out a set of parallel practice tracks in the instruction area on the flat, with one crossing track for the instructor/teacher. Here is where you will demonstrate, practice, and review the techniques to be used in striding the trails.

If you have a nearby hill that you can use, all the better. Lay out a trail to the hilltop or a point 400 to 600 meters up the slope. From that point down, lay out a variety of downhill runs, each involving a natural or man-made terrain formation demanding specific

maneuvers, such as turns, bicycle dips, roller-coaster dips, snow bumps, and various combinations.

If you are really cramped for space, you can lay out practice tracks in ovals or figure eights around your basic instruction area.

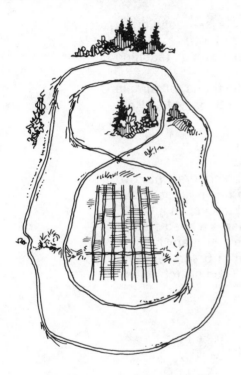

Always lay out a learning area to promote activity; keep the kids moving. Don't make them wait for anything is the golden rule of good cross-country ski instruction.

In one respect teaching cross-country skiing demands more of an instructor/teacher than does the teaching of Alpine skiing or ski jumping. In those ski disciplines, the excitement of performance — speed, technique and balance — is a great motivation. The rewards are less obvious in cross-country. So in teaching cross-country it's often the instructor/teacher that has to provide the spark that motivates, through a good choice of teaching situations and skiing experiences.

Games are, of course, fun, but they must be chosen with care. For example, traditional games often have many instructional drawbacks when played on skis, because:

- Equipment can be damaged.
- Often only a few children play at a time, while others are inactive.
- They often don't promote ski techniques; children may run as if on foot.
- Non-instructive games waste teaching time.

However, on-ski modifications of simple games can have high instructional value. Here are four of our favorites:

Hare and hounds. Divide the children into two groups; one hares, the other hounds. Have them ski in parallel sets of tracks, about 30 to 40 meters long. Give the hares a head start of three meters or so, and see how many hounds catch the hares (by tagging) before passing the "free" line at the end. Then switch roles.

Parallel tracks, about two hand widths, 8 inches, apart.

Cats and Dogs. Divide the children into two groups; one cats, the other dogs. Use the same tracks as for **Hares and Hounds**, but line the "cats" and "dogs" up in two parallel rows about ten feet apart, with their skis across the tracks. Give a start command to one of the groups: if you call out "Cats!" the cats have to turn their skis into the tracks and "catch" the dogs before they get away, and vice versa. This exercise builds the ability to turn rapidly in either direction.

Pole chase: Have the group start together from a starting line, skiing parallel tracks 30 to 40 meters long to a finish line. At the finish line, there are poles stuck in the snow, one fewer than the number of children starting. The pole-less child at the end of a "heat" sets up the poles for the next chase.

100-130 FT.

Tag: Simply an on-snow version of the all-time favorite. Lay out a circular track with a couple of cutoffs, where all children have to ski the same direction. The "it" player can be cap-less, as shown here. Upon being tagged, a player gives up his/her cap, and becomes the pursuer.

ABOUT 80 FT.

6 FT.

THE DIAGONAL STRIDE

The diagonal stride is fundamental in cross-country skiing. A good diagonal stride is characterized by rhythm, efficient kicks, active poling maneuvers, and gliding on one ski at a time. It resembles and is a further development of the basic strides of Chapter 1. The refinements include sharpened kick efficiency for longer glides, and a displacement of maximum leg and arm work relative to each other; the longer the glide, the greater the displacement.

Kick

Speedy skiing effects short, impulsive kicks, which, in turn, are what produce the characteristic diagonal stride.

A good kick depends on good ski grip on the underlying snow. So a kick can be thought of as having two parts, **sink** and **push**. First the trailing leg comes rapidly forward and there's a slight bend, or **sink** in the knees, which increases pressure on the underlying snow and stops leg motion for an instant. Then there's a forceful forward **push**, starting with a hip extension and followed by knee and ankle extensions. The kick finishes when the kicking leg is fully stretched, a trailing extension of the upper body lean. The sign of a good kick is that it is short and forceful, resulting in a marked glide.

Sink! The ski grips the snow.

A six year-old with a good kick.

Glide

Good glide requires full weight shift. As shown in the sequence below, when there's a kick on the right (frames 3 and 4), the left ski glides forward and weight shifts smoothly from the right to the left ski. Weight transfer is complete (frame 5) when the kick finishes. The skier then glides on a single ski, and the trailing leg first swings rearwards and up, and then forward in preparation for the next kick (frames 4 through 6). The sign of a good glide is that its final phase is all on one ski.

A good diagonal stride by a six year-old wearing ordinary touring skis, fitted with heel-strap bindings, and high touring boots.

Poling

A poling maneuver usually starts with a pole plant beside the forward foot, with arm extended forward (frame 5 of sequence above). Then the arm **pulls** on the pole (frames 5 and 6) until it passes the hips, and then **pushes** (frame 6). The maneuver finishes with pole and arm in a straight line, from shoulder to pole basket (frame 1). After the active, propulsive phase, the arm and pole swing forward (frames 1 through 5); the hand and arm start and steer this pendulum swing during the glide phase.

A short wrist loop and relaxed fingers — the push goes through the loop. The hand opens towards the end of the pole push.

Balance

Good balance is the very foundation of good technique. Technique itself can be learned through copying others and through being instructed and corrected. But balance cannot be learned in the same way. Skiers gain balance only through experience in gliding on skis in a variety of ways — on one ski and on both skis — through thousands of repetitions. In Chapter 1 we reviewed the learning of balance (page 29); there are no shortcuts to learning it. Balance is acquired unconsciously, and is more or less picked up as one learns technique.

The Learning Situation

TERRAIN

Cross-country skiing maneuvers may be used anywhere there is snow, but they are most easily learned in tracks. Therefore tracks are an essential part of the cross-country learning area. If possible, learning area tracks should be firm and settled, a day or more old, and should have a side area packed out for poling. The tracks don't have to be set by machines; in fact, skied-out tracks are usually better. This is because most track setters are designed to set tracks for use by adults; the track spacing is too broad and the depth too deep for use by children. So in skiing out tracks, keep this in mind, and set tracks for your youngsters, not yourself.

Skis

Skis must grip and glide well to be useful in a learning situation. The pupils might grapple with new techniques, but they should never have to fight their skis. So always spot check ski grip and glide before you start the day's activities. Waxable skis should be waxed well, and waxless skis should be clean. Initially, ski grip is most important. But as the skiers gain proficiency, they'll probably find grip easy and want more ski glide. Then it's best to wax for more glide, or, for waxless skis, to treat the bases for glide.

PRACTICE

Some of the glide practice exercises of Chapter 1 (page 38) may also be used for practicing balance. Skating strides are especially useful if skis are slippery or grip is poor. The same games (page 39) may also be used to imbue basic glide skills. Here are some additional practice games suited to the learning area loop tracks, such as those shown on page 70.

■ SPEED
Ski the 600-meter loop faster than you normally ski.

■ QUICK AND RIGHT
Ski the shorter 200-meter loop:
- As fast as you can without running as if you were on foot.
- Fast, with forceful kicks so you feel the glide between kicks.

■ HOW FAR
Count how many times you ski the loops.
- How far did you ski during today's class?
- How far have you skied in classes so far this season?

COMMON LEARNING PROBLEMS AND GUIDANCE EXAMPLES

● **UNRHYTHMICAL STRIDE**
Evident as uncoordinated arm and leg work.
Typical problems are shown in sequences I
and III below; a good correction is shown in
sequence IV.

All pole work ahead of the body disrupts
rhythm in sequence I above. Compare the
first and third frames here with frame 2 of
sequence IV.
- Avoid firm, fixed grip on poles. Relax
  fingers.
- Try poling by pushing only, with poles behind the body.
- Swing arms and poles up in back.
On a slight downhill:
- Pole as if skiing the diagonal stride, but
  without kicks (sequence II).

II

Using only one ski pole, on a slight down-hill:

• Ski, aiming for a full poling motion.
When using only one pole, it's difficult not
to pole rhythmically.

III

Stride rhythm can be broken when arms and
legs on the same side work almost together,
as shown in sequence III above. Compare
the problem of position 2 with the better
stance of position 2 of sequence IV.

• Cheer as you ski: "WE SKI!" for each kick;
  "WE!" on the sink, "SKI...!" on the push,
  feeling the full stretch, one hand forward,
  the other back. Try the maneuver on a
  slight uphill track; the resistance of the
  slope aids learning rhythm.

• Ski speedily and powerfully up a slope.

IV

WE

SKI

1   2

Chant to get the rhythm:
"WE SKI !!!"

● WEAK KICKS

Weak kicks result in little obvious glide. Skiers often stride rapidly, working all the time with no resting glides.
•How fast can you ski 100 yards?
On a track going from a flat up a slight slope:
•Can you ski as fast, or faster up the slope than on the flat?
•Try a pole-less scooter-kick stride.

V

1   2   3   4   5   6   7

The scooter-kick exercise may be done with or without a ski on the kicking foot (shown above). The exercise is good practice for the glide position (frames 6 and 7) and lets the skier get the feel of how a good kick (frame 5) gives forward power.

NOTE FOR THE DOWNHILLS

In skiing back downhill from the slight uphill stride exercises, have the skiers assume the In skiing back downhill from the slight uphill stride exercises, have the skiers assume the Telemark position so they can practice a valuable maneuver on the way back downhill.

● SHORT STRIDES

Amputated strides often occur with excessive up-down body bobbing.
•How few kicks can you use to ski to the end of a given track?

VI

1　　　**2**　　　**3**

- Try the scooter-kick, shown in sequence V above, to get the feel of good ankle bend on the gliding foot as part of the kick to follow (compare frame 5 of sequence V with frame 2 of sequence VI).
- You're kicking up. Try to push yourself forward.
- Pretend that you're skiing fast, but hidden behind a low fence, so nobody sees you.

● TWO-SKI GLIDE

Gliding on two skis after a kick is usually caused by the body being too far in back of the forward, gliding foot.

- Where's your weight when you glide? Put pressure on that forward ski!
- You toe your way forward. Try to get that knee forward, over the foot.

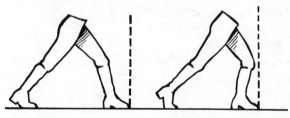

Wrong:
Foot forward.　　　*Right: Knee*
　　　　　　　　and foot forward.

- Pretend that you are going to dribble a soccer ball with your forward, gliding foot, cradling the ball with your ankle.

- **BACKWARD BUTT**

  Sitting back towards the end of a glide and during the initial sink phase of a kick robs the skier of forward power.
  - Like the late kick, this problem is difficult for the skier to detect or "feel," as it occurs in a fraction of a second. The best cure is to have the skier ski in a good track up a slight hill, at high tempo. Chances are the backward butt will then come forward.

THE UPHILL DIAGONAL STRIDE

The uphill diagonal stride is basically the same as the diagonal stride on the flat. But there are a few differences, because:
- The kick must provide both forward power and power to lift the skier up the hill.
- Skis slip backwards more easily on hills than they do on flats.

The results are that:
- The steeper the hill, the shorter the glide.
- Tempo is higher than on the flat.

Technique changes accordingly; obviously affected are the grip and the push of the kick, and pole work.

1. **Grip part of the kick.** As the steepness of the slope increases, glide diminishes, and there's less of the characteristic sink in the knees at the start of each kick. To get good ski grip, the leading foot comes farther forward than in the equivalent position on the flat (frame 1). This permits a forceful kick that can bring the body forward over the opposite ski to apply pressure for the next kick. The result is:

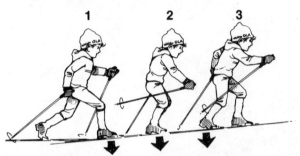

   - The kicking ski applies pressure nearly perpendicularly to the snow (1).
   - The lack of knee sink to initiate the kick is offset by the ski being weighted on the snow over a relatively longer period of time.

   A weak kick results in the trailing ski coming down on the snow and being weighted too soon, which takes pressure away from the kicking ski, where it's needed.

2. **Push part of the kick.** Strides are shorter because glide is less and tempo is greater than on the flat. Therefore the upper body is more vertical than when skiing on the flat.

3. **Pole work** is also affected by the need to lift the body vertically and by the greater chance for ski backslip.
   - Arms bend more for greater power.
   - Poles are planted farther behind the forward foot (frame 1 above).
   - The first pull phase of poling is far more powerful than the final push phase (as can be seen in the finish of the right-arm poling of frame 1 above).

The Learning Situation

TERRAIN

Lay out several tracks up a range of slopes from gentle to steeper, starting from a flat. The easiest hill should be so gentle that all skiers in the group can ski up with a good glide in their diagonal stride.

PRACTICE

The skiers ski up various uphill tracks, maintaining their glides as long as possible without breaking rhythm. Chances are if they ski a good diagonal stride on the flat, they will automatically alter their strides to suit the hills. What's important is that they get a feeling for the hills and for how they have altered their flat-terrain strides to suit the slopes. **Careful with any instruction of the differences for their own sake!**

COMMON LEARNING PROBLEMS AND GUIDANCE EXAMPLES

- **RUNNING**
  Skiers run (as if on foot) uphill when they could glide.
  - Try to keep your glide going as long as possible up the hill.

- **BACKSLIP**
  - Emphatically weight that kicking foot on uphills!

On steeper uphills:
- **SLAP**

    The trailing ski slaps down on the snow just after the kick, as shown here (frames 1 and 2). The cause is usually that the body is back, in a sitting position (frames 2 and 3).

1   **2**   **3**

SLAP!

- Hear the slap? Ski so you don't hear it!
- Feel that trailing leg swing past the kicking leg.
- Lean well into each kick; feel that lean.

    If the skis still slap:
- Put more power in your poling to give your skis better grip.

HERRINGBONE

The uphill herringbone rhythmically resembles the uphill diagonal stride, but differs in that the ski tips are spread into a V. Therefore, pole plants are farther out to the side and slightly farther back. The steeper the hill, the broader the spread of the ski tips.

The Learning Situation

TERRAIN

Set a firm track from a flat up a hill of gradually increasing slope so the skiers will have to shift into a herringbone to ascend the hill.

DOUBLE POLING

As shown in the sequence here, double poling can be done with (frames 1 through 6) or without (frames 7 through 12) a leg kick. In both forms the arms and upper body supply most of the forward power.

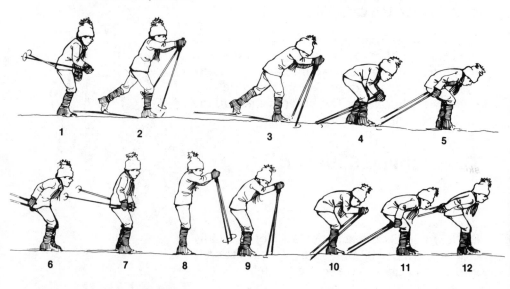

1   2   3   4   5

6   7   8   9   10   11   12

In straight double poling, the arms swing forward in unison, and poles are planted with baskets even with each other (frames 5 through 9). Arms then pull (frames 10 and 11) and push (frames 11 and 12) on the poles. A slight elbow bend and forward weighting by the upper body add power to the arm work (frames 9 and 10).

The push (frame 11) finishes when the poles and arms are in a straight line (frame 12). Then the body rises and the poles swing forward for a new pole plant (frame 6, 7, 8).

Double poling with a kick, the **double-pole stride**, is more powerful and therefore is used when straight double-poling is ineffective. A double-pole stride starts with a kick (frame 1 and 2); the double-poling then starts (frame 3) and finishes, and the arms swing forward (frame 6 and 7). Two kick strides may also be taken between successive pole plantings.

Uses

Double-poling is most used when skiing at speed through terrain variations.

A kick in a dip (left) followed by double poling let the skier bound ahead, as if from a trampoline. Double poling at the crest of a hill (right) gives speed for the downhill to follow.

Also, as repetitive motion is tiring, double-poling is actually a relaxing variation to diagonal striding on a trail. Just when and where to switch depends on ski glide and the slope of the track.

Changing strides is best done at fair skiing speeds, or when speed will increase, such as at the crest of a downhill. When cresting a downhill, the double pole plant is timed just as skis start to glide downhill. The rhythm of a change is like a double-pole stride with two strides.

For stride efficiency, arms and poles should come forward during a kick (frames 1 and 2 of double-poling sequence) and the trailing leg should come forward when poling power is maximum (frames 3 to 5 of double-poling sequence).

The Learning Situation

TERRAIN

Set firm tracks, preferably from a slight downhill out onto a flat, so the skiers can diagonal stride back to the start. Otherwise, the general layout is like that for the diagonal stride. Set a few tracks over bumps, or make bumps in tracks if need be, and set a few over crests of downhills.

PRACTICE

- **HOW FAR?**
  How far can you ski with ten double-polings?

- **HOW MUCH?**
  Can you double-pole 50 feet up a slight uphill?

- **RHYTHM**
  Alternate between kicks and double-polings, commanding yourself rhythmically: "KICK! POLE! KICK! POLE!"

- **ALTERED RHYTHM**
  As for RHYTHM, but with two kicks: "KICK, KICK! POLE!"

- **VARIATIONS**
  Combine RHYTHM and ALTERED RHYTHM.

- **BUMPS AND DIPS**
  Ski downhill through terrain variations, such as the dips and bumps shown below. Absorb bumps with the legs, and keep the body well forward.

COMMON LEARNING PROBLEMS AND GUIDANCE EXAMPLES

- **ARMS ONLY**

  Skiers don't use their upper bodies for double-poling power.
  - Lean over your poles, and curl at the waist as in a situp.
  - Feel your chest "pushing" when your arms are all the way down.
  - Is your weight on your poles?

- **POLE PUSH CUTOFF**

  As shown in the sequence below, the amputated poling maneuver is characterized by the push finishing too early, followed by an early body rise as the poles come forward. Compare the first three frames of this sequence with frames 5 through 7 of the double-poling sequence on page 84.

| 1 | 2 | 3 | 4 |

  - Complete that push! Feel that your arms swing up in back after poling!
  - More power in your poling; finish each poling with a snap!

● UNRHYTHMIC DOUBLE-POLE STRIDE

As shown here, the poles come forward earlier than they should with respect to the kick timing; compare frames 1 and 2 with frames 1 and 2 of the double-poling sequence on page 84.

1   2   3   4   5   6

- Get the rhythm by commanding yourself: "KICK!, DOUBLE-POLE, KICK!, DOUBLE-POLE."

● LATE LEG TIMING

The ideal time for the trailing leg to come forward is when arm and upper body pole push is greatest, as shown in frames 3-5 of the double-poling sequence on page 84. Bringing the leg forward later is less efficient, as seen in frames 3-6 above.
- Let that back leg trail until you feel your poles biting the snow!
- Swing that leg forward when your arms are pushing hardest!

● DOWNSIDE DOUBLE-POLING

Double poling on the downside of bumps actually wastes energy, robbing the skier of a chance to rest while gliding.
- Double-pole on the crest of the bump, not afterwards!
- Kick before double-poling so you get the most out of the downside! (As shown on page 85.)

CHANGING DIRECTIONS

All tracks and trails change directions, and no two changes are alike. There are curves and turns on the flat, on uphills and on downhills, and they vary in sharpness and length. So there are many ways to turn. The step turn and skate turn, described in Chapter 1, can be used in a variety of cross-country skiing situations. Gliding turns, which rely more on skier speed than on any propulsive maneuver on the part of the skier, are also part of Alpine ski technique, so we discuss them in Chapter 3.

Skate Turn

The skate turn differs from the step turn in that it is an accelerating turn. It is usually done between two tracks that meet each other at an angle, and is typically a single skating step between two double polings. Here the skier glides on both skis in the old track (1) as after a double poling with arms swinging forward. With weight on the outer ski, he lifts the inner ski in the new direction (2), and pushes on the outer ski to land on the inner ski in the new track (3), with arms now fully forward. The maneuver finishes with a new double poling (4).

The Learning Situation

TERRAIN

Use the same type of learning area as used for double poling. Set up branches or poles in the snow to mark where the skiers should turn without running into each other. Lay out figure-eight tracks for skiers who have good kicks and weight shift; they can practice skate turning to both the left and the right. Lay out a variety of track intersections or turns that can be negotiated at a variety of speeds, and make some of them sharp enough to require skating steps.

PRACTICE

- **AT THE MARKERS**
  Ski downhill and change directions at the markers.

- **FIGURE EIGHT**
  Ski a figure-eight track, speeding up while changing direction.

- **THE WOODS**
  Set up a maze of poles on a flat, and challenge the skiers to skate through "the woods" without stopping.

COMMON LEARNING PROBLEMS AND GUIDANCE EXAMPLES

- **WEAK KICK**
  If the kick on the outside ski that powers the turn is weak, it's usually because the skier's balance is not yet good enough to master the maneuver. In this case, practicing the turn itself is useless as the necessary basic

skills aren't there. Instead, practice skating in a specific, smaller area.
- Skate as if wearing roller skates or ice skates, ahead and to the side. Try to skate a bit uphill too.

But some skiers have the balance; for them try:
- Crouch a bit more before leaping in that new direction.
- Your kick goes up, not forward! Feel that the knee of the inner leg is well bent before you kick.
- Try to kick to push yourself forward in the new direction!

A good skating turn: inside knee bent and a kick pushing in the new direction.

- **KICK-FOOT SLIP**
  - Feel the inner edge of that outer ski dig into the snow before you kick!

The Crooked Trail

Good skate turns require power and balance, both of which take time to build. A crooked trail that requires practice of these skills will speed their learning, and teach the skiers how to master terrain.

Start with a crooked track laid out in relatively flat terrain. Put in as many changes of directions as you think the skiers can manage in the terrain — around trees, under bridges, in dips, around buildings and the like. In meeting the challenge of skiing a crooked trail, they will learn some of the joys of free skiing.

STRAIGHT DOWNHILL RUNNING POSITIONS I: PACKED SLOPES

Running straight downhill is common to all skiing—cross-country, Alpine, and ski jumping. The joy of speed is an excitement that most kids cannot resist, so you seldom have to work hard to convince any young skier to take a downhill run.

Stable position of readiness.

There are three general stances for skiing downhill. The nearly fully erect **position of readiness** is a stable, dependable position. But it offers the most air resistance, which slows speed. The **crouch** offers less air resistance, and also can be a resting position, with elbows against knees. Still lower is the **egg**, the position offering the least air resistance.

The crouch: easy, with elbows resting against knees.

The Learning Situation

TERRAIN

Select and pack a hill, or a broad area down a hill, ending out on a flat long enough so the skiers can stop without having to turn. If possible, find or pack out a few downhill terrain variations, such as roller-coaster dips, bicycle dips, series of small bumps, and so on. Mark uphill tracks to be skied with uphill diagonal and herringbone strides on either side of the downhill area.

The egg: low, with upper body parallel to snow, knees springy and bent, arms slightly bent and close in to poles in direction of motion.

Practice

- **BUMPS**

  Ski downhill over bumps and dips, in an egg position if possible. Make yourself light going up on a bump (pull your legs up under your body), and heavy on the downside of the bump (pushing your skis down against the snow).

> **■ WASHBOARD**
> Ski over a series of small bumps. Pretend that you are a car driving on the washboard surface of a back road. How good are your springs?

COMMON LEARNING PROBLEMS AND GUIDANCE EXAMPLES

- **UNSTABLE AND STIFF**
  The skier is unstable; the body stance is stiff, and the skis are together.
  - Ski with your skis hip-width apart.
  - Try to be stiff and see what it does to your balance. Think relaxed!

- **THE WADDLE**
  Some skiers try to get low from the hips down only; they waddle downhill.
  - Try skiing slower; lift your hips and lower your torso, as if "protecting" it against the wind.

STRAIGHT DOWNHILL RUNNING POSITIONS II: VARYING TERRAIN AND VARYING SNOW

Skiing downhill as the terrain and snow surface varies is an art in itself. Mastering this art is one of the joys of wilderness skiing.

The best all-round stance is the stable position of readiness, preferably with one ski about a boot length in front of the other, and most of the weight on the trailing ski. This

Good balance in skiing varying snows.

position can help prevent a fall if the skis break through crust and the back weighting helps keep the skis up on top of the snow. In skiing into a dip or sudden rise it's often most stable to go into the Telemark position, with several boot lengths between the feet and the knees at an extreme bend. This is a good position to meet varying snows, especially for skiing fast from hard snow into loose snow.

Telemark position in a sharp transition.

The Learning Situation

TERRAIN

Seek natural variations as much as possible; it's a whale of a job to make them yourself. Besides, the natural are the most realistic. Look for varying slopes and snow conditions typical of what your skiers may meet on a cross-country ski tour where they ski.

Telemark position skiing from packed to loose snow.

PRACTICE

- **DIPS**

  Ski downhill through dips. Start in a position of readiness, feet nearly alongside each other, and then go into more of a Telemark position, with weight well back when you ski into the dips.

- **SNOW CHANGE**

  Ski from hardpack into loose snow, weight back when skiing into the loose snow, so skis ride up.

WILDERNESS RUNS

Skiing downhill on any slope frequented by skiers will seem simple if you ever ski downhill on true wilderness runs, where you never know what's coming next. Wilderness runs are where the terrain really teaches, and where quick reactions and mastery of a broad range of skiing maneuvers count. Not all cross-country skiers will be wilderness skiers, but a bit of the excitement of skiing the unexpected peps up advanced classes.

Meeting the unexpected with a jump to the side.

The Learning Situation

Try to find a patch of wilderness to ski, however small. It should have slopes and flats, bumps, turns of many types, and dips. If the patch you have available doesn't have enough excitement of its own, you can go out in advance, preferably when there's a bit of wet snow that will pack easily, and build your own terrain variations. In skiing your wilderness, have the skiers start at different places, according to their abilities.

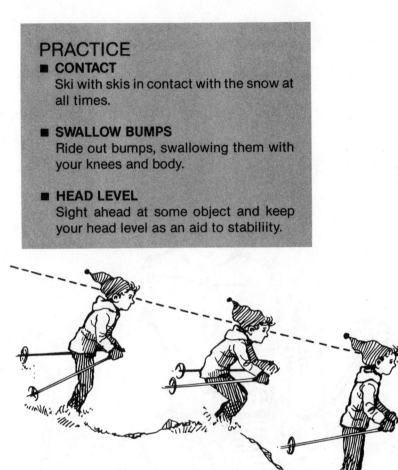

AND NOW MORE

Cross-country skiing isn't just a set of on-snow exercises; it's a key to enjoying winter in ways not otherwise possible. Your skiers should learn this basic joy as they learn the techniques of cross-country. Take them on tours; even impromptu, shorter tours during classes. You may be surprised how much their technique will improve if something catches their interest. While they are learning the ski techniques that will enable them to explore winter wilderness, let them find out what that wilderness has to offer.

3 ALPINE SKIING

The focus of this Chapter is on developing maneuvering skills for downhill skiing terrains. But these skills aren't restricted to use on hills served by tows and lifts. They are useful to skiers of any bent, in all sorts of downhill situations. The grouping under the heading **Alpine Skiing** distinguishes the various maneuvers from those of flat and uphill skiing (Chapter 2 on Cross Country) and those involved in flight (Chapter 4 on ski jumping).

Skiers use downhill skiing skills in many ways. Some ultimately want to ski beautifully, others fast. Intricate maneuvers on packed hills may appeal to some, while simpler maneuvers on remote mountain slopes will appeal to others. Recreational lift-hill skiing, slalom racing, freestyle, ski ballet, cross-country downhill, and wilderness skiing can all develop naturally from the same broad base of downhill skiing proficiency. Therefore our approach here is geared to provide that broad base, building on the basic universal skills of Chapter 1.

This approach contradicts several of the current stylized schools of Alpine skiing instruction. But if you compare the illustrations of this chapter, showing proficient youngsters skiing, with photos of today's top Alpine ski racers, you'll find the similarities amazing. It's as if the racing world has recently discovered what it's like to be little. The no-nonsense, effective way proficient children execute Alpine skiing maneuvers should be emulated, not tampered with.

WHAT MAKES A TURN

Unfortunately, the language of Alpine skiing hasn't yet settled down. No two books on the subject agree completely in their descriptions of what goes on in the various downhill skiing turns, and they frequently disagree on the very names of the turns. Sometimes, slight modifications of older turns reappear in new dress with a new name, particularly if they are introduced from another country speaking another language. So we'll start by defining the way we view downhill ski turns. A skier turns by **edge shifting, turning,** and **controlling** the skis. These are not isolated components, but rather essential parts of the rhythmic whole of a turn. They are so dependent on each other that you must be experienced to single out and observe the action of any one of them.

Turns And Edging

Turns are continuous changes of direction. As shown here, they may be made on **unmatched edges** or **matched edges** of the two skis. **Matched** means that both right edges or both left edges of the skis are involved. Turns on **unmatched edges** include the basic snowplow turn and the initial phase of the stem Christie turn, in which the turn is executed on the inside ski edges, one right and one left. All the more advanced and more effective turns are made on **matched edges**. In a left turn, for instance, this means that the left edges of both skis are active in initiating and carrying through the turn. Between successive left and right linked turns, the skier performs an **edge change**. The motions of and balance in edge changes are difficult for beginners to learn. Edge changes are always initiated by some body movement, called an **edge change movement**.

Both skis shift edges in completing a turn. Therefore, a turn may involve either two separate shifts, one on each ski, or a single simultaneous shift on both skis. Think of the difference by likening a series of linked turns to a piece of music, with one turn per musical measure. The rhythm is either dual, with two accented musical beats (edge shifts) per measure, or single, with only one accented beat per measure.

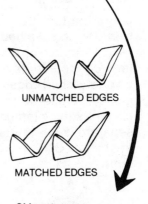

UNMATCHED EDGES

MATCHED EDGES

Skiers turn on unmatched edges (top) or matched edges (bottom) of their skis.

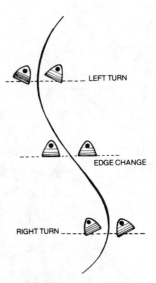

LEFT TURN

EDGE CHANGE

RIGHT TURN

Edge changing in single-shift rhythm: a left turn on left edges followed by simultaneous edge shifts on both skis and a right turn on right edges.

Edge change movements in **dual-shift rhythm** are involved in all turns where the skis are on unmatched edges. Typical is the stem Christie, shown here to the left. The skier starts the turn from a position in which both skis are on **matched** (right) edges. The right ski is stemmed up and out, and shifted onto its left edge to initiate the turn. The skis are now on **unmatched** edges. In the turn, the left ski is closed parallel to the right ski, and the right ski shifts to its left edge. There have been two separate edge shifts in the turn, in a dual rhythm of "ONE, TWO!"; **right-ski shift, left-ski shift.**

Dual edge-shift rhythm: Turn starts with skis on right edges (1). The first shift is on the right ski, which is stepped uphill and rolled over to its left edge (2). The skier is then on unlike edges (3). The final, second shift is on the left ski, so the skier finishes the turn on like edges (4).

Edge-change movements in **single-shift rhythm** are most obvious in all the various forms of parallel turns, including parallel turns initiated by a skating step.

A five-year-old using single edge-shift rhythm starts a turn on matched edges (1), shifts edges on both skis simultaneously (2), and finishes turn on matched edges (3).

THE CHOICE

Children naturally adapt to turning with edge-change movements in single-shift rhythm, and easily learn it if they can make a good snowplow turn.

Children who can change edges in the single-shift rhythm can easily learn to shift edges using the dual-shift rhythm. But the converse isn't as easy: children accustomed to executing turns by changing edges in the dual-shift rhythm have difficulty learning the single-shift rhythm. This difficulty, along with the ultimate goal of skilled Alpine skiing — to ski with skis parallel (which requires edge change movements in single-shift rhythm) — are the basic for the first basic rule:

> **Basic Rule I: Edge changing in single edge-shift rhythm is best.**

TURNING

Turning describes the way the body moves to power a turn.

Obviously, the skis and the skier interact in all turns. First, all modern skis (with the exception of cross-country racing skis, which children learning to turn should not be using) have sidecuts. When a sidecut ski is banked on an edge in snow, it will carve an arc in the snow. If skis glide, sideslipping at an angle to their length, they also tend to follow a curved path. In both cases, the features of the ski have produced turning.

In their first turns, children should simply learn to use these elementary turning features of their skis. So in the beginning, their skis determine how sharply they can turn.

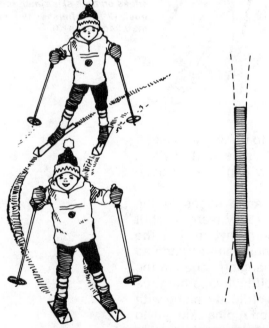

Sidecut on a ski aids turning.

Here's a six-year-old turning with skis in a broad stance. Note that the tracks are small; there's little sideslip. The skis determine most of the arc of the turn, and the rest is produced by the feet steering the skis.

If the skier is to determine the arc of the turn, **axial motion** of the body must be used. There are two main types of motion around the body's axis, **rotation** and **counter-rotation.**

Rotation: The upper body and/or the hips twist in the direction of the turn, and the torsion brings the skis around.

Counter-rotation: Torsion is applied to the skis, and the body reacts with torsion in the opposite direction, or counter rotates.

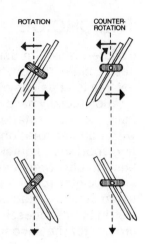

Both rotation and counter-rotation can swivel skis.

Here's a nine year-old skiing a wide-track Christy turn, using counter-rotation. He's not using any special Alpine ski gear, just sturdy over-ankle cross-country ski boots and cable bindings on broad touring skis.

A good Christy by a nine year-old.

THE CHOICE

Children who turn using counter-rotation can easily learn to turn using rotation. But the reverse isn't as easy: children who turn using rotation usually have difficulty learning to turn using counter-rotation. This difficulty, along with counter-rotation's advantage of permitting shorter and quicker turns, means that it's best that children learn counter-rotation first.

In counter-rotation, the upper body appears to remain fairly stable while the knees lead the skis in their successive turns. This is the background for the second basic rule:

Basic Rule II: The legs turn the skis.

This type of turning works best with the body low, down to a squat. Then the calves follow the twists of the feet. In higher stances, the hips also follow. What's important is that the torsion producing the turn is best produced in a low position, which allows rapid and efficient ski turning.

Control

The body leans inward in a turn, which produces edging, the adjusting of the angle between the bases of the skis and the underlying snow.

A skier exercises this control mainly with the foot and by transverse motion of the knees, in or out to make sharper or longer turns. The knees can be moved in this manner only if they are bent. So **bent knees** are one of the primary marks of a good skier.

Knee and hip work go together. The hips are free to work well when they are directly over the heels and the upper body leans slightly forward.

Knees and ankles bent (left) and hip bend angulation (right) promote control of skis.

With the hips in one place, the knees can move underneath to control the skis, but only through a limited sideways angle. So it's the hips that provide the overall, rough control, and the knees and feet that provide the final, fine control. Hip control work can easily be seen in the sideways angulation, or bend at the hips. This leads to the third basic rule:

Basic Rule III: The position of control is marked by bent knees and angled hips.

THE CHRISTY

The **Christy** is a skis-parallel turn involving forward sideslip. Its name is a contraction of **Christiania**, which, up to 1924, was the name of Oslo, the capital of Norway.

The Christy and its many variations are by far the most used turns in skilled recreational downhill skiing. Christy turns may be done slowly or quickly; they may be long or sharp; and they may be done with skis practically glued to each other or with skis at a wide stance.

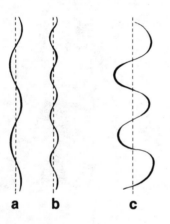

The Christy is used for long turns (a), short turns (b) close to (a, b) or well across (c) the fall-line of the hill.

a   b   c

Broad Is Best for Kids

Children will always try to feel secure and stable on their skis. So their natural downhill ski position is with skis fairly far apart—the **wide stance**.

Following Basic Rule I, the turns are best made using the single edge-shift rhythm. When skiing in a wide stance, this is most easily done if the turns are slight arcs, close to the fall-line of the hill.

According to Basic Rule II, the turns should be made using counter-rotation. Children tend to use rotation if they have to make sharp turns while skiing in a wide stance. So again, it's best to start with turns close to the fall-line.

The Wide-Stance Christy

The wide-stance Christy is a turn past the fall-line using forward sideslip, with skis parallel or nearly parallel, fairly far apart. The wide-stance Christy is the first major advancement in the progression from the basic snowplow turn, which involves turning on opposite edges, to true finished turns involving single-edge-shift rhythm.

Here's a wide-stance Christy done well by a nine year-old. Note that edges change at the same time on both skis, and that the boy has good counter-rotation and control over his skis.

The Learning Situation

TERRAIN

Pick a gentle, even, well-packed slope that permits skiers to ski at different speeds according to their abilities. Mark off courses with markers.

PRACTICE

Starting with a snowplow turn which they can do, most children will automatically gradually switch over to the wide-stance Christy when performing maneuvers that favor its use. We recommend this natural transition.

■ **SPEEDY PLOW**
Who can ski fast making snowplow turns?
Adding the challenge of speed produces more body lean towards the inside of each turn, much as children automatically learn how to lean a bicycle more on higher-speed turns.

This five year-old's long plow turns will soon become finished turns.

MARKERS CHALLENGE AND AID

You can build the challenge of terrain into even the easiest of slopes and also aid the instruction of maneuvers by marking off courses or areas with poles, traffic cones, or even dog dishes.

Poles: Best are those used for Alpine ski races, as they are easily planted in the snow and don't bend or shatter when hit by a skier. They are available at most Alpine ski areas, but you can always fashion makeshift poles from tree branches, plastic tubing and the like. Poles are so useful as a learning aid that we'll say more about their uses later, starting on page 136.

Traffic cones are the hollow, free-standing, rubber or plastic, inverted-funnel-shaped markers used by police and street crews to temporarily mark off lanes, access to toll plazas, detours and the like. We recommend them for a beginner learning area. They can be easily and rapidly set out or moved, and they allow greater freedom of arm movement than do poles, as children can ski close to them and clear their tops with their arms. They flex and give when hit by a skier, they are light, and they stack and store well. You can probably fit enough of them for marking your area into the trunk of a car.

Dog dishes made of flexible plastic or molded rubber are an inexpensive and readily-available alternative to traffic cones. They are usually available in different sizes and a rainbow of colors (although two colors are enough for a learning area), and you can probably fit enough in a backpack to mark off a good-sized area.

Here's a five-year-old skiing a plow turn at higher speed. Because of the speed, the ski tips are wider apart, the skis sideslip less, and weight is more on the outer than on the inner ski of the turn. The child is well on the way to a wide-stance Christy, as can be seen by the child's steering with the outer foot and knee and the body position with hips over the skis.

● **LOTS OF TURNS**
How many turns can you make from the top to the bottom?

Here's a child in a speedy snowplow turn. Note the marked outside leg work in the middle of the turn (frame 2); the inner ski doesn't contribute much support or control, so it's flat on the snow.

● ZIG-ZAG

Ski between the markers. Start three feet farther up the hill on each run.

Offset markers, such as the traffic cones shown here, on either side of the fall-line, to clear skis in the wide stance.

As shown here, because the skiers ski with a wide stance, the markers are placed in a zig-zag to guide turns close to the fall-line.

This exercise helps the skiers to turn:
● Rhythymically, with the finish of one turn begin the start of the next.
● Close to the fall-line, which requires little turning of the skis, which in turn favors counter-rotation.
● At specific places, which demands greater control and edging of the outer ski.

Skiers who practice in this manner will learn to flatten their inner ski and gradually shift to using its inside edge. This is not an isolated change, but rather a natural part of faster skiing that leads to changing edges in the single-shift rhythm.

A good Christy with edges shifted together.

Here's just such a case: a child skiing on left edges in a left turn (1) and right edges in a right turn (3). He's doing a wide-stance Christy. The edge change from left to right occurs just as the two turns link together (2). Note that this does **not** mean that the edges dig, or the skis bank into the snow by exactly the same amount at the same time; the inner ski can be banked or set later than the outer ski. Here the **short swing** rhythm is useful to drill in edge change and control, and counter-rotation body position. Keep the upper body and hips supple to hinder rotation.

COMMON LEARNING PROBLEMS AND GUIDANCE EXAMPLES

● WEDGE CHANGE

The angle, or wedge, of the snowplow changes with direction, which can retard learning single edge-shift rhythm.

- Can you ski all the way with your skis in the same wedge?
- You're pushing out on your skis; try to keep them at the same distance.

If necessary, set up markers to limit outside ski sideslip.

● ROTATION

Rotation with turns from turn to turn.

- Crouch a bit, as if facing a wind blowing up the hill; don't lean upper body over. Face chest downhill all the way!
  Rotation disappears if turns are tightly linked.

- Stand downhill and signal turns with a pole, or set markers 50 to 100 feet apart and challenge skiers to make as many turns as they can between the markers.
- Ski without poles, with a longer marking pole across bent arms. Ski so the pole is steady across the hill, not rocking.
- Pretend that the long pole is a kayak paddle: a dip and a stroke on the left turns the "kayak" to the right and vice-versa.

● HIPS OUT

Hips out in a turn blocks hip angulation and prevents effective edging.

As seen in the turn above, hips out often occurs together with rotation. So work first to eliminate the rotation. If that doesn't bring the hips in, try:

On a slight slope:

- Turn just slightly, near the fall-line, with no upper body follow-through.
- Take hands out of pole straps and hold poles crosswise in front of body, stretching them horizontally to the far outside of each turn.
- Again without ski poles, hold long pole across shoulders, behind neck; pole should point down and back to outside ski on each turn. NOTE: this is a potentially hazardous maneuver should the skier fall or collide with other skiers, so arrange it with great care.
- Pretend that you're in water up to your neck; ski so your shoulders don't break the water surface.

On a modified zig-zag course:
Set up inward inclined poles at each marker so skier will shy away from them at each turn.
- How close can you ski to the markers?

Sometimes a swayed lower back fixes the hips, preventing angulation. Straightening the sway may free the hips:
- Try to arch your back when you ski. Be a cross cat!

● OUTER FOOT STRETCH

Considerable ski edging, rough and stiff movements.
- Ski light as a feather.
- Ski so you don't make tracks in the snow.

● HANG-BACK

Hanging too far back is often the cause of other problems.
- Try skating and skate turning.
- Try jumping as you turn: get those ski tails off the snow!
- Try skiing on one ski in a turn: the outer, or maybe the inner ski.

● EXCESSIVE BOBBING

Overdoing a turn, with up-unweighting and excessive edging is a minor problem, often a sign that skier's skills have advanced beyond those needed for the turn.
- Ski so the pompom on your knit cap doesn't bounce!
- You stand up between turns. Can you try to go down instead?
- Ski over a bump or mogul and turn on its top. Keep eyeline roughly level; bend your knees to "swallow" the bump.

Set up gates using two ski poles and a crosswise ski pole on top of a series of bumps/moguls on the slope.
- Ski through the gates and turn at them. Don't lean the upper body over too much!

The more the skier leans into the turn with good body angulation, the closer the hips are to the hill (distance A, above). Keeping the skis in contact with the snow requires the skier to keep hips low. This in turn requires a marked knee bend, or down-unweighting to shift edges (as indicated by distance B, above). This technique provides superb control of the skis from the initial phase of a turn, up until the skis cross the fall-line.

SOME GOALS

A good wide-stance Christy turn has all the fundamental components of the more polished, finished turns of Alpine ski technique. Progress comes through skiing terrains of increasing difficulty, skiing at higher speeds, making faster turns, and turning more sharply from the fall-line. However, skiers should not be pushed beyond their abilities, into skiing situations where they fall back upon separate ski edging. They should keep good technique habits, such as edging skis together, as they progress.

Some forward sideslip is part of all Christy turns, but forward sideslip itself should not be encouraged. Turns follow curves, while sideslipping slows speed. Good skiers sideslip as little as possible; they control speed by controlling the arc of their turns.

The goal is **carved turns**, or turns executed with a minimum of sideslip. Again, the reason for the goal concerns the skier's future total turn capabilities: the skier who can carve a turn has no trouble tossing in some sideslip, which may be needed to brake speed. But the skier who is accustomed to executing all turns through sideslipping often has great difficulty learning to carve turns.

In other words: sideslipping is a vital skill: for braking speed or checking, but not for turning.

Here's a five-year-old boy doing a couple of very decent linked Christies on a gentle, packed slope:

Note the boy's long turns, the edging of both skis together with a minimum of movement, the good body position with knees bent and ambulation at the hip, and the low stance, with the outer shoulder down, providing excellent contact between skis and snow. The boy's skis have steel edges, but he's wearing ordinary sturdy touring boots with heel strap bindings. That is, his heels aren't held down to the skis and he isn't wearing special Alpine boots or bindings.

THE STEM CHRISTY

The Stem Christy turn combines the stem turn and the pure Christy turn. It is done with separate ski edging, and is useful on steeper slopes.

Here's a good stem Christy starting from a traverse (1). The upper ski is stemmed out and shifted onto its inside edge to initiate the turn (2). The skier plows in the fall-line on unlike edges (3), and then closes skis together, with the second edge shift on the inner ski (4) to continue with skis parallel.

Plow turns are difficult on steeper slopes, because the skier tends to slide downhill before a turn can be completed. Also, the inner ski in a turn is banked on its inner edge, which can catch and run in the snow, causing the legs to spread and the skier to lose control.

Wide-stance Christies are also difficult on steep slopes for skiers who have previously used them only on fairly gentle slopes where they can fully control speed. They can make long-arc turns fairly straight downhill without applying much power on the gentle slopes, but may not be able to transfer that capability to steeper slopes and higher speeds. They usually aren't proficient enough or powerful enough to control speed with sharp turns using the wide-stance Christy technique.

Control is the major factor in the ability to turn on steeper slopes. This is why beginners often go into a plow position in initiating turns on steep slopes, so as to control speed when it's greatest, just as the skis point downhill. Keeping the inner ski free is the most important part of the last phase of the turn, so here the parallel ski stance is best.

The Learning Situation

TERRAIN

Pick a slope so steep that the group can barely manage it skiing plow turns. Use poles or markers to mark off turn directions.

PRACTICE

■ **GARLAND**
Repeat plow Christies several times in succession, in the same direction. Start with a plow (frames 1 and 2 above), and turn and close the inner ski to the outer ski (frame 3). Then try the opposite direction.

■ **LINKED TURNS**
Link several stem Christies and work on shortening the stem phase.

■ SLALOM

Mark places to turn with poles, far enough from the fall-line so skiers don't need to sideslip to check. The "course" may also be laid out at a downward angle to the fall-line.

■ SHORTER TURNS

Start with long turns and gradually make them shorter.

COMMON LEARNING PROBLEMS AND GUIDANCE EXAMPLES

● LOSS OF CONTROL

Excessive edging on the inner ski prevents sideslip and the skier speeds up.
- Stay in the plow position until you cross the fall-line!
- You roll your skis a bit too much up on their edges. Can you keep your skis just as flat on the snow as you do in the plow turn?

● ROTATION

The skier initiates turns with rotation frequently only in turns to one side, such as the right turn shown here.

- Keep your chest facing downhill as you turn!
- Look downwards towards the tail of the outside ski when you turn the inside ski.
- Hold both ski poles vertical, in front of the body. In a right turn, twist so both poles move towards the tail of the left ski, and vice versa.

● BODY ERECT IN EDGE SHIFT

Rotation and upward movement often occur together.
- Bend your knees more; keep that low position.
- Keep the usual body position in the plow phase of the turn and sink down as the inner ski turns.

SIDESLIP CHECK

A good rule for downhill skiing is that the skier should control the speed; the speed should not control the skier. Controlling speed means that the skier should be able to check or stop at any time to avoid an accident or collision.

The most efficient way of checking is to sideslip, to a complete stop if necessary. The decelerating force of the maneuver is greater for skis more perpendicular to skier motion and for skis more on edge. Aside from being an excellent and necessary maneuver, the sideslip check is excellent practice in counter-rotation and in controlling edge changes together.

From a straight downhill run, the skier checks by powerfully pulling skis across the fall-line to a sideslip stop. The body reacts with counter rotation, and the low stance aids the maneuver; only the legs turn with the skis. After the stop, the skier still faces the original direction of motion.

The Learning Situation

TERRAIN

Pick a slope steep enough for the highest downhill speed the skiers can handle comfortably. Poles can be used to mark off a corridor for stopping.

PRACTICE

- **HOW SOON?**
  How soon can you stop from:
  - A traverse?
  - Skiing straight down the hill?
- **HOW CLOSE?**
  Set out small twigs or other small markers several places on the hill.
  - How close can you ski to the marker and sideslip to a stop without touching it?
- **HOW QUICKLY**
  The skiers ski downhill, thrust their skis into a sideslip and stop on command.
  - How quickly can you stop?

COMMON LEARNING PROBLEMS AND GUIDANCE EXAMPLES

● **NOT ENOUGH TURNING**

The skis don't turn enough, so the sideslip doesn't stop the skier, but results in a downward sliding traverse. Set up a corridor of poles, broad to begin with.

- Start fast, and try to stop completely without skiing out of the corridor.
- Be emphatic in turning the skis into the sideslip.
- Repeat turning, on top of a bump or mogul.

Turning on top of a bump or mogul offers little resistance to ski swivel under the feet, while turning on the flat or in a dip offers great resistance.

● **HIP ROTATION**

The hip swings sideways and out in a turn.

- Ski downhill in a wide stance, fairly erect, and turn skis to a stop upon command.
- Can you stop quickly and still keep your butt uphill?

Other problems: Other body motions, such as rotation and turning one ski at a time, can be used to initiate a sideslip. Skiers may find them easy and therefore use them, but they are not as efficient or as rapid as the straight counter rotation sideslip check, which is actually the simplest maneuver. Rotation and separate edge changing have their places, but they shouldn't be used as substitutes for the more basic maneuvers involving counter rotation and simultaneous edge change on both skis.

THE TELEMARK TURN

Historically, the Telemark turn is the oldest downhill ski turn. It was one of the standard turns for Alpine skiers during the development of the sport, before lifts became common. In 1941 the U.S. Second-Class skier test required four linked Telemark turns. The turn is, as it always has been, one of the reliables for cross-country wilderness skiers. And it is now enjoying a competitive renaissance, as the turn for a newer type of slalom race. Telemark turns, many skiers maintain, aren't just useful — they're a lot of fun.

Although modern "Telemarking races" are held on packed slopes, the Telemark turn is basically a steered turn for deep snow. The basic principle is that a curved object will tend to follow a curved path. This is why the ski position of the Telemark turn, which approximates a long curve, is responsible for the turning involved.

To start the turn from a skis-parallel traverse position, the outer ski is advanced and weighted, being brought forward and around by the outer knee and hip. The inner ski carries less weight, and its tip is about even with the boot of the outer ski. The skier shown here spreads his arms wide for balance.

The Learning Situation

TERRAIN

Preferably an even slope with a good snow base and four or five inches of new, light snow.

PRACTICE

■ **POLE SUPPORT FOR A START**
Start, preferably, from the fall-line of the hill and turn to whichever side you wish, or find easiest, initially supporting the start of each turn by planting your poles in the snow for balance.

■ **NO POLES**
Make the same turn, but without the initial pole plant.

■ **THE OTHER WAY**
Repeat the above, but in the other direction.

■ **LINKED**
Ski linked Telemark turns down the hill.

SKI TRICKS AND EXERCISES AND A BIT OF FREESTYLE

Ski tricks and exercises sharpen downhill skiing skills and vary the routines of maneuvers. Most have direct and obvious value, and you'll seldom have trouble persuading a gang of eager kids on skis to do any of them. In fact, if your classes are not strictly regimented (as they should not be), then you'll probably see some of the following tricks and exercises with no prompting at all. Some of them are borrowed from freestyle skiing; just being able to do them adds a new dimension to the joy of downhill skiing.

Sit-back-to-egg

Ski straight downhill and vary stance from low crouch to egg.

Sit-back-to-tip-touch

Ski straight downhill, alternating hands on ski tails with hands on ski tips.

Lie-back-to-squat

Ski straight downhill, alternating stance from extreme lie-back to squat.

Shift back-to-front

Ski straight downhill, alternating extreme "hanging back" in bindings with forward lean. This maneuver requires Alpine-type bindings that hold heels down.

Downhill change

Ski straight downhill, alternating crouch and egg downhill positions.

Charleston

Rapid short-swing turns on the inside ski; kicking the underweighted ski tail out adds the Charleston dance touch.

Hinge hop

Rhythmically hop, lifting ski tails, leaving tips on the snow.

Geländesprung

The Geländesprung (German for **terrain jump**) is a small upward and forward jump, with a double pole assist. Also try tucking knees upward when jumping.

Crouch short swing

Ski short swing turns in an extreme crouch, holding poles at their middles.

Jet turn

Most often done with feet swiveling on a bump; poles planted laterally downhill, body weight is fairly well back on the skis.

Outrigger

A turn on the inner ski with the unweighted outer ski far out to the side.

Reul Christy

This is a one-legged Christy on the inside ski. The outer leg and ski are raised, up and back.

Single ski Christy

This is single-ski short swing, with the other foot ski-less.

Inside Christy

A pronounced lean to the inside weights the inner ski for a long turn with the outside ski unweighted, off the snow.

POLES AS AIDS

Poles on a slope are a challenge to any skier, and to children they are almost irresistible. They don't have to be used in a disciplined racing layout, and you don't have to know anything about Alpine ski race courses to benefit from their use. A small course is fine for challenging the desire to compete, and we'll talk a bit about setting up courses. But first and foremost, poles are superb learning aids.

Pick a pole length long enough that if a skier falls against the pole, its length flattened on the snow is longer than the skier is tall; this avoids hazards of being hit by the whipping pole end.

Pick pole materials that are non-hazardous to the skier in falls. Best in this respect are the newer gate poles made for marking Alpine ski racing courses, as they whip and bend, but seldom break. Poles made from fairly green tree branches also work well. Bamboo, particularly old bamboo, can splinter if hit hard, but tends to flex at a fracture instead of breaking off. Avoid poles made from fiberglass-polyester tubing; they often fracture by breaking off, leaving sharp ends. If in doubt, break a few of the poles you intend to use and think of what might happen should a skier fall on that break.

Poles are most visible, and most interesting for children if they are brightly colored. Painting poles may be a chore, but unpainted poles can sometimes fail to achieve their purpose. Think, for instance, of the visibility of a pole made from a birch branch, stuck into the snow with a birch grove in the background. On an overcast day with flat light, it will be practically invisible.

Finally, pick light poles that you can carry, transport, store and set out easily. No sense making too great a chore for yourself before class begins.

Poles cannot change a hill, but when set up to define a course for skiers they change the terrain as seen and experienced by the skiers. Even the most humdrum slope can leap to an exciting life through careful pole placement that challenges skier abilities.

So poles aid learning in two general ways: first as a sort of signposting for specific new and/or corrective practice maneuvers, and second as a sort of artificial terrain feature to sharpen skills. Examples of these types of uses follow; you can vary them and perhaps concoct many more to suit your specific learning area situation.

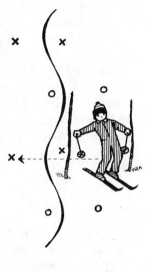

To promote hip angulation and knee bend set pairs of poles as "gates" for long turns to either side of the fall-line. For hip angulation, stretch upper body towards outer pole of a gate. For knee bend, bend knee nearest outer pole in initiating a turn.

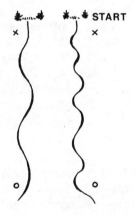

To promote counter-rotation and shifting edges together set up two pairs of poles fairly far apart down the fall-line, so several turns may be done between the pairs. Challenge the skiers to see how many turns they can do between the two gates. Vary the exercise by having them start farther uphill from the first gate, so they ski faster, or by varying the distance between the gates.

To promote counter-rotation mark out a right and a left turn with poles. Have the skiers ski turns downhill from the poles with their backs to the poles (a), or uphill from the poles extending their torsos towards the poles (b).

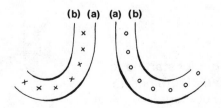

(b) (a) (a) (b)

Natural slalom: Slalom as a competitive event grew out of the oldtime impromptu ski races downhill through wooded terrain, where real trees were the "gates." Here's a modern version, far less hazardous to the skier in case of miscalculation — a forest of poles on a slope. Set the poles up about two ski lengths apart. Challenge the skiers to ski through the forest in as many ways as possible. See if they can remember how they turn by asking them to ski the same route twice. Then see if they appreciate how they turn by asking them to find two routes that require totally different ways of turning or turning rhythms.

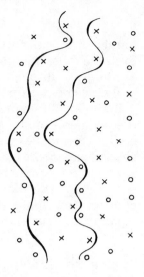

Arches promote relaxed stance and cure rotation: Set up archway gates low enough that they require good knee bends for the skiers to pass. About 25 to 30 feet between gates is suitable. Arches are self instructive in promoting a relaxed stance, because skiers can't be too stiff as they bend their knees to get through the arches. The cure for rotation takes a bit of understanding: have the skiers turn with their backs, not their chests towards the inner pole of each turn.

Turn on bumps or moguls for rapid, counter-rotation turns. Many skiers turn relatively slowly, using rotation, because they find turning is difficult. Making turns easy can speed them up and cure the rotation. Do this by setting up a series of poles near bump or mogul crests, so the skiers can turn by swiveling on the crests.

This is also a good practice run for starting to learn inside pole plant for quick turning; it's easiest on the top of a bump or mogul.

Cure lingering rotation by upping turn speed so there isn't enough time to rotate. Do this by placing a second pole downhill from each of the poles on the bumps/moguls to form a gate through which the skiers must turn.

To cure the upward body straightening that often accompanies rotation, set low "gateways," using two vertical and one horizontal pole at each bump/mogul top. In skiing and turning under the horizontal poles, the skiers must have a low stance with knees well bent. This is also good practice for mogul skiing.

To promote like, carved turns to both sides set up a series of poles along the inside of arcs of linked downhill turns. Excess sideslipping or asymmetrical right-left turning will throw the skier off the course and out of sync for the following turn. Have the skiers ski the course until they manage to follow it all the way through.

To cure one-sided rotation and promote correct edging set up a line of poles at an angle to the fall-line, at spacings of about two ski lengths. Pick the angle of the line, right or left as you face downhill, so the skier turns downhill from poles in the troublesome direction. Have them keep their backs to these poles when skiing, and ski with good knee bend. Such lines are self-instructive on edging, as repeated turns on a downhill traverse simply cannot be made without good edge control.

The poles can be placed farther apart than indicated in the sketch here.

Parallel Slalom is always popular: neck and neck, skier against skier, just like the pros on TV! Pick an even slope and set up parallel rows of poles straight down the hill, picking pole arrangement and spacing to suit the maneuvers to be practiced. Here are a few of our favorites:

Round the pole: Have the skiers ski completely around some or all of the poles of a course. Start with an easy arrangement. Shown here on the left is a course where the skiers ski around double sets of poles, but otherwise just ski around each pole. Then have them ski around each pole of a course, as shown on the right. To make it more interesting, have the skiers start slightly downhill from the first set of poles so they must ski uphill a bit, by skating, herringboning or sidestepping, to make their first turns.

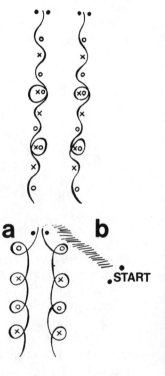

Pole dancing down the hill — rhythmic turning just like the pros race — is great for practicing all-round balance and proficiency. Set up parallel rows of poles, about 12 to 15 feet apart. You can set poles at even spacings, as shown in (a) to promote rhythm in short-swing turns, or at uneven spacings, as shown in (b) to promote ability to continually change turn rhythm. The third course (c) is like the second (b), but it has poles placed farther apart for greater course speed.

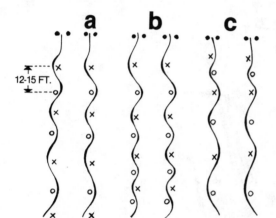

To promote shorter turns set up a funnel-shaped corridor of poles. Skiers start at the top with longer turns; in the funnel they can gain rhythm, progressively shortening their turns towards the bottom. The course may be set up so the skiers turn inside all poles, or are allowed to turn outside alternating poles.

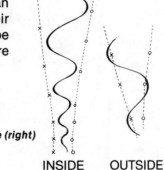

Skiers can turn inside (left) or outside (right) of a funnel.

INSIDE   OUTSIDE

To promote sideslip checking/stopping set up
two parallel rows of poles down the hill to form
a corridor. Skiers ski into the corridor and turn
to a sideslip at the first set of poles. How fast
can they stop, by which pole? This arrangement is self-instructive, because skiers who
fail to check properly will ski off course,
past one of the rows of poles.

To promote skate/step turns set up a course that does not require checking or stopping, but requires control of speed. This tends to promote skate turning because the turn can be made sharp without loss of speed, which is why it is now so frequently used in slalom races. Single poles in a row are enough of a challenge for this exercise, as children will most frequently turn by a pole, any pole, even if they could otherwise have skied straight downhill. So exploit their natural turning tendencies in setting up a demanding skate turning course. Simple rows of poles, 25 to 40 feet apart will do, with alternating poles on alternate sides of the fall-line. A slight offset, shown on the left, encourages straight running between poles, with skate turning around each pole. A greater offset, shown on the right, encourages carved turning along with the skate turning.

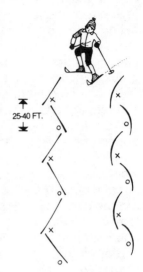

To promote judgment in turning set up two rows of poles down the hill, about 10 to 15 feet apart, with about 15 feet between the poles. The skiers can ski inside the "corridor" formed by the poles, around each pole of each of the rows, or successively around alternate poles of alternate rows, as shown here. Set a closely-spaced pair of poles at the top of the course so skiers may ski out of it, making their first turn to the right or to the left.

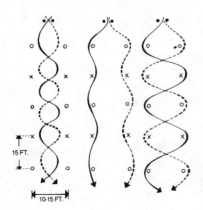

Turns may be made inside a corridor (left), along each of its rows (middle), or around poles of alternating rows (right).

SLALOM COURSES

Skiing slalom courses has value beyond enjoyment or the awakening of the competitive skiing spirit in children. Because turns must be made where the course demands them, a slalom course builds the ability to react quickly in downhill skiing situations. Quick reactions on the hill are the key to enjoyable, challenging and safe free skiing

Slalom can easily be overdone, however, and, regrettably, it often is — much to the dismay of well-meaning parents or instructors, who see their children lose interest in the sport simply because they are weary of the regimented skiing required by slalom. So slalom should never be a goal in itself; free skiing and command of a hill are always preferable.

Slalom courses consist of **gates**, each formed by a pair of poles. There are three basic types of gates: the **oblique** at a downward angle to the fall-line, the **open** across the hill, and the **closed** along the fall-line. These three simple gate types can be combined to form gates requiring more than one turn, such as the **hairpin**, a combination of two successive closed gates, and the **flush**, which is a hairpin plus an additional closed gate.

For competitive slalom courses for adult skiers, gates are set with poles 10½ to 12 feet apart. For children, the poles may be set closer, about two ski lengths apart. If you have blue and red poles to lay out a course with, set consecutive gates in that color order: blue, red, to conform to slalom racing rules. There's nothing like adding a dash of racing realism to your course.

In setting courses, strive for challenge but not for restriction. Tough, restrictive courses may be all right for the best skiers in a racing situation, but for most skiers they frequently degrade technique and retard learning progress, causing skiers to "fight" the course and fall into bad skiing habits while so doing. If you see this trend in your group, it's time to stop racing and start a bit of free skiing. Then, on the sly, re-set the course

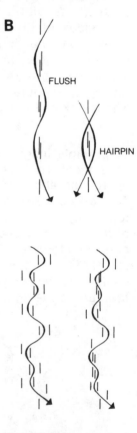

A

The three basic two-pole slalom gates, oblique, open, and closed, and the two closed gate combinations, the hairpin and the flush, can be used to set a wide variety of courses.

B

How different courses can be skied the same way. The course on the left is set with open gates, while the one on the right has both open and closed gates.

AND NOW MORE

Encourage free skiing whenever possible, with skiers alone and in pairs. They should practice rhythmic linked turns of like arc and length, leaving the narrowest possible turn tracks in the snow. Pick terrain that challenges the group's capabilities, but emphasizes good edging, carved turning, and independent leg work. The terrain will then teach the skiers to blend into the hill and not fight it.

Edge control and turn carving are part of free skiing.

Separate leg work builds ability for precision skiing.

As anyone who has ever taught knows, teaching and instructing are superb learning situations for one's self. So whenever possible, put one or more children in charge. Have them set up a small slalom course; have them ski follow-the-leader behind each other; have them ski in particular ways down a hill. In challenging each other they often forget the hill is there, and just ski it. And that's your goal.

The perfect jump at a meet, the roar of the crowd — or the dream of flying?

4 SKI JUMPING

Given the chance to jump on skis, almost any child will jump, for the sheer thrill of the experience. The question then is: what can they learn from it? The answer is **plenty:** jumping and much more!

Just as the downhill ski turn skills grouped under Alpine skiing in Chapter 3 are used by all skiers on downhills, the skills of ski jumping are useful to any skier who becomes airborne. Ski jumping skills are useful to any skier who succumbs to the temptation to jump off of bumps, knolls, cornices, or moguls on a downhill run.

Every Skier an Icarus

The thrill of being airborne, and perhaps a fleeting realization of the age-old Icarus dream of wings, is there to be had by all who jump. And we believe that in any young skier nothing can replace the experience for the thrill involved. That's why this chapter emphasizes the flight experience of jumping for boys and girls.

We emphasize boys **and** girls to underscore that ski jumping skills are definitely not only for the development of future competitive ski jumpers. That's a sport in itself, a game for men only, developed far beyond the basic skills of this book. So for the ski jumpers of this chapter, the thrill of jumping is available at a level that knows no sex barriers. Jumping not only adds excitement and enjoyment to classes, but builds general skiing proficiency. It should therefore be one of the more important parts of skiing for beginners.

Close Ties

Even skiers who never jump owe something to ski jumping and may actually practice many of its maneuvers. This is because ski jumping has long had a far-reaching influence on the overall development of the sport of skiing.

Through the years, maneuvers and techniques originally developed by ski jumpers have been adapted to other skiing purposes. The **Christy** turn of Alpine skiing and the **Telemark** turn, now the standby of "Norpine" cross-country downhill skiing, were both originated by ski jumpers, as ways to turn to a stop after landing. The low-profile crouch used on downhills was also first developed by ski jumpers, for highest inrun speed before taking off into the air.

WHAT'S IN A JUMP

All jumps involve flight, getting the skis off the underlying snow for a distance, however short or long. To the skier jumping and to anyone watching, the flight is the focus of the maneuver. So we'll start by saying a few words about flight.

First, true aerodynamic flight and long jumps are the stuff of competitive ski jumping. As we've said, that's a sport by itself. Its relation to the kind of jumping we're talking about here is about the same as that of circus acrobats or stuntmen diving off high structures to dives into a backyard swimming pool. The principles may be similar, but the scales are vastly different.

For instance, simple jumps can be done off a mogul or a "kicker" jump where there's a steeper downhill section to land on. Although flights on these jumps are short, kids can get the feel of acrobatic control in the air. They can:

- Do a split, legs spread and arms wide.
- "Pedal" with the legs, as if cycling.
- Twist, swiveling the upper body first one way, then the other.

Split

Swivel

They can also perform many of the traditional maneuvers of ski jumping. Three favorites, from the ski jumping of a century ago, are the erect stance, the tuck, and the Telemark landing. They are shown here drawn from old photos, taken when gentlemen jumpers wore full peasant costumes, including hats and sheath knives. All three maneuvers originated in the Morgedal district of Telemark county, Norway, in the latter half of the last Century.

The erect stance is a ramrod, arms-spread in-flight position.

The tuck is what the old-time ski jumpers most often did after taking off from a **sprit-hopp**. As in broad jumping, the idea is to pull legs up for distance.

The Telemark is a bent-knees position, with one ski trailing the other at about half a ski length. Some say it looks like genuflecting on skis. It is used both to cushion the shock of landing and to turn at the end of an outrun.

Erect stance.

Tuck.

Telemark landing.

SKI JUMPS

A "real hill" will do the most to capture interest and motivate youngsters to learn jumping.
By "real" we don't mean **big**. By "real" we
mean a hill with a good starting place, a well-
packed inrun with a stable track, a well-
prepared knoll, a straight section, a transition
and an outrun. Because jumping capability
and desire varies greatly among children, it's
best to have two or more jumps of different
sizes, so everyone can jump according to their
ability.

Build the jump wide for safety. The transition
between the inrun and the takeoff section of
the jump should be smooth, and the last few
yards of the takeoff section should be horizontal. Select the direction of the jump with
relation to the slope of the hill to minimize the
pressure of landing after a jump. For the same
reason, avoid extending a jump takeoff so far
down the hill that the skiers land in the transition of its outrun. Space the inrun tracks about
a fist-width apart, and pack them as hard as
possible.

The knoll, or first convex part of the profile
of the hill after the takeoff, should start at
about the same inclination as the takeoff. The
height difference between the knoll and the
takeoff should be enough to allow jumpers to
jump about three to six feet and still glide well
down the hill. The knoll and the following
slope of the jump should be slightly convex.

The overall slope should be rather gentle instead of too steep. The transition should run smoothly out to a following flat outrun. The outrun, transition, and knoll should be packed hard, so ski tracks and uneven snow surfaces don't cause falls.

If you've never built a ski jump before or would simply like to have further information, contact your regional or national ski association for details.* The information they can supply is extensive, and mostly directed towards building large hills for competitive ski jumping, but it usually includes many useful tricks of the trade applicable to even the smallest of hills.

A WORD ON GEAR

The skills of this Chapter can be learned (and are shown demonstrated) by children shod with sturdy, broader cross-country touring skis, boots and bindings. As a safety measure, poles are not used in jumping from ski jumps. The only piece of special gear we would ever recommend for beginning child jumpers eager to take up the sport would be slightly longer and broader touring skis than they customarily use, or perhaps an old pair of shorter Alpine skis (with their steel edges either removed, filed completely round, or covered completely for safety's sake).

Bindings should allow maximum forward foot flex while holding the heel firmly and preventing sideways boot slip. The heel cable/strap cross-country binding is best in this respect, but the sturdier pin bindings can also be used.

Boots should allow foot freedom while supporting the ankle. Most important, they should allow lacing so they fit firmly and don't come off by themselves.

---

*The national ski associations in both Canada and the U.S.A. are organized in regional geographic divisions; contact headquarters for further details:

Canadian Ski Association
333 River Road, Tower A
Vanier, Ontario K1L 8B9
tel.: (613) 746-0060

United States Ski Association
1726 Champa Street, Suite 300
Denver, Colorado 80302
tel.: (303) 825-9183

INRUN/
INRUN POSITION   SPRING

FLIGHT

SMALL HILL JUMPING

Unfortunately, the word "jump" means both the flight through the air and the entire performance. So from here on, we'll be specific, speaking of the entire performance and dividing it up into its four consecutive phases: **inrun, takeoff, flight,** and **landing and outrun.**

Just as the height of a high jump or the length of a broad jump are themselves goals, the length of a ski jump is important for most who jump. Length depends mostly on the speed at takeoff, the timing of the spring at takeoff, the power in the spring, and the jumper's poise in the air. Think of these factors in any analysis you might make of a single phase of jumping.

Inrun

A speedy start is the key to good inrun speed, so something for the skiers to butt their ski tails against or push off from is an aid in starting. Lacking any fixed object, they can take three or four diagonal strides down the hill to pick up speed. After that, their speed is determined by how streamlined a body position they hold and how well their skis are

TELEMARK LANDING

A good hill counts, but it isn't decisive. Here a thirteen year-old executes a nearly perfect jump on a fairly flat jumping hill.

waxed. The earmarks of a good inrun position are:

- Weight carried equally on both feet, at hip width apart.
- Knees apart, forward shin pressure on boots (ankles bent).
- Upper body parallel with skis.
- Torso rests in contact with thighs.
- Shoulders relaxed, with arms loosely extended back.

Takeoff

The **spring** at the takeoff is what brings the jumper from the inrun position to the in-flight poise. A good spring controls the entire rest of the jump. It should bring the jumper rapidly into flight poise, so as to retain as much inrun speed as possible, for maximum flight length.

A good spring is a little "explosion" on the lip of the jump that pushes the jumper up and out. Think of it as being as **late** as possible with respect to the lip of the jump. The extension in the knee and hip joints is rapid and major, while the extension in the ankles is minor, and completed along with the final knee extension after the jumper has passed the lip of the jump.

The lower legs retain their angle to the skis on a good takeoff, and then the upper body comes rapidly forward, over the skis.

Flight

In-flight body poise is not decisive for shorter jumps, up to 50 to 65 feet or so. The body should be extended, with a slight forward hip bend, a sort of "banana profile."

The arms should be held close in to the body, with hands flat at natural arm length below the hips. Skis should point upwards, slightly above the horizontal, and be parallel, about a fist width apart.

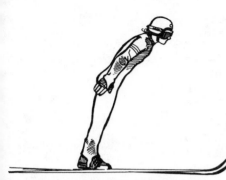

A top international ski jumper in flight in a
25-foot jump (above) and a 325-foot jump (right);

the flight poise of World Champs isn't always
flat over skis.

Landing and Outrun

A good flight ends with a Telemark-position
landing. The Telemark position is best
because it cushions the shock of landing and
because it enables the jumper to handle the
deceleration as the skis come onto the snow
and to quickly deflect the sharp changes of direction from flight to landing to skiing the
outrun.

As late as possible at the end of the flight,
the arms should move from the along-sides
flight position out to a balance position. One
ski should move ahead of the other by about
the length of the jumper's calf. The forward
knee should lead the forward ankle slightly,
and the rear knee should be near the forward
ankle. The landing puts the most pressure on
the forward foot.

Once safely landed, the jumper stands
slightly more erect and skis the outrun with
bent knees — sometimes with one ahead of
the other in the Telemark position — and then
turns to a stop at the end of the outrun.

LEARNING THE SKILLS

Takeoffs and landings are the skills to be learned on small hills. Those who take up ski jumping seriously later will build on these basic skills when they go to bigger hills. Those who occasionally seek the air in other types of skiing, or simply want not to fear it, need to know how to get up into it and down out of it with control and, in some cases, grace. In terms of safety, landing is the most important aspect of ski jumping. It's easy to get skiers up into the air, and it often happens unintentionally on downhill runs. But it takes skill and confidence to land, and lack of that confidence can cause fear and apprehension in flight, on the takeoff, or before. And that fear itself can be a hazard, causing the skier to "freeze" in a poor position during a jump. So to counteract the **fear of landing**, we put landing first, ahead of all other jumping maneuvers. It should be the first learned and most frequently practiced.

TELEMARK LANDING

A **Telemark landing** isn't just a position the skier gets into. It is a complete and continuous fluid motion that cushions the shock of landing, absorbs the body weight, and deflects the various changes of direction from flight in air to glide on snow. Other landing stances are possible and are used, but none are as eminently suited to the task as the Telemark landing.

Typical "sitdown landing" by a beginner who hasn't learned the Telmark landing.

The Learning Situation

TERRAIN

There is no one type of terrain for learning the Telemark stance and Telemark landings. There are many; for instance:

- On downhills, after practicing uphill diagonal stride
- On slight slopes
- On downhills on practice loop tracks
- On ski tours
- On long, gentle downhills

Upon scanning the above list you may immediately react: "Hey! Where's the ski jump? Isn't that where they need to land?"

To that we say "true, all too true." But it won't take you more than a couple of sessions with a gang of eager kids on a jump to convince you of the futility of teaching basic landing technique there. Most often, the kids couldn't care less as they are absorbed in the excitement of takeoff and flight. Here it's best to surrender and let the kids be kids. So see that the drills to automate landing skills happen elsewhere.

PRACTICE

There's no set routine for learning Telemark landings, so the following six exercises are not ordered in any progression. Use them as suits the skier's abilities and interests.

■ **IN PLACE**
Jump up, and land in the Telemark position in place. Most skiers will put their jumping foot forward.

■ CHANGE

Alternate between erect stance and falling into a Telemark stance, in place.

■ GLIDING

Practice Telemark positions on downhill runs, on loop tracks, or the like.

■ UP-DOWN

Change between erect downhill stance and Telemark stance while gliding downhill.

■ SMALL SPRING

Spring up and then land in Telemark position, on a downhill run.

■ POLE ASSIST

Same as SMALL SPRING, but with a pole-assisted takeoff to get up into the air.

COMMON LEARNING PROBLEMS AND GUIDANCE EXAMPLES

- **WEIGHT BACK**
  The skier weights the rear foot and has little fore-aft spread between feet.
  - Try the position in place; feel the pressure on the forward ski.
  - Push the rear ski so far back that the knee is near the leading ankle.

Weight back, legs close landing.

- **EXCESS FORWARD BEND**
  - Feel that your chest/upper body is erect.
  - Is your chest forward?
  - Ski in Telemark position balancing a snowball on your head; it will tell you how you're standing on your skis.
  - Feel the difference between "the bow" (excess forward bend) and the kneeling Telemark position.

Upper body too far forward.

INRUN AND TAKEOFF

Although inrun positon has little effect on jump length for jumps up to about 50 feet on beginner hills, it's important to learn it as a part of overall jumping capability. The spring at the takeoff is the single most important maneuver in a jump. It takes time to acquire the precision, directional control, and timing necessary for a good spring.

The Learning Situation

TERRAIN

The same general learning terrain as used for landings can be used for practicing inruns and takeoffs. If you have a long, gentle downhill available, try marking it off with branches or markers every 25 to 30 feet. The skiers can spring for takeoff at each marker, and land in the Telemark landing before the next marker, and then resume an inrun position for the next takeoff.

Pine branches placed across hill mark successive takeoff points.

PRACTICE

The following seven exercises are arranged in order of increasing difficulty, not as a progression to be followed in learning, but rather as an aid to providing exercises for skiers of differing abilities.

■ **INRUN IN PLACE**
  - Keep knees apart.
  - Upper body rests against thighs.
  - The head is a natural extension of the back and the neck.
  - Hips up until upper body is about parallel with skis.
  - Arms relaxed and back, parallel with skis.
  - Position is soft yet ready, like a cat prepared to jump.

Good inrun position.

■ **SIMULATION IN PLACE**
  Like INRUN IN PLACE, but alternated rhythmically with rising up to an erect stance, and sinking to a Telemark position. Shift hip height to get a feel for proper hip height in relation to head.

■ SIMULATION IN MOTION
Like SIMULATION IN PLACE, but done when gliding in a firm, wide stance.

■ SIMULATION WITH A SPRING
Like SIMULATION IN MOTION, but with a spring lifting ski tips off the snow. Stay loose until landing. Resume inrun position after Telemark landing position.

■ MINI JUMP
Like SIMULATION WITH A SPRING, but done taking off from three or four very small jumps on a downhill slope. Attempt smooth takeoffs for stable outrun skiing.

■ A REAL HILL
Like MINI JUMP, but done off a small jumping hill. Spring is still weak. Retain supple cat-like readiness as long as possible up to the jump lip.

■ JUMPING
Like a REAL HILL, but now with full spring on takeoff. Remember the cat ready to jump and be cat-like. Don't bull your way off the jump.

COMMON LEARNING PROBLEMS AND GUIDANCE EXAMPLES

● STRAINED STANCE
A strained inrun stance is often caused by poor balance or by apprehension and fear of the oncoming flight and landing. SO IT'S VITAL THAT THE SKIERS JUMP A LOT BEFORE GUIDANCE IS GIVEN TO OVERCOME THE PROBLEM.

- Knees at shoulder width; chest in contact with thighs.
- Head down and forward, a natural extension of back and neck.

Stiff, "open" inrun position. Note: raised head, shoulders down and stiff, no bow in back, and knees often together.

● HIGH STANCE
- Guidance as above for STRAINED STANCE

● SPRING TOO EARLY
Timing the spring is the most difficult task in jumping. A correct spring is actually a **late** spring. Here **late** means that the legs are not fully extended until the skier has passed the lip of the jump.
- Stay in the inrun position of readiness until you feel the underlying support of the jump inrun disappear under your feet.
- Get lower on the inrun; the lower you are, the farther you've got to go.
- Spread some loose snow on the takeoff. Can the skier "leave heel prints" in that snow?
- How long can you stay in a squat before you spring?

Early spring, with knees extended completely before jumper reaches lip of jump, forces ski tips down in air (left), while correct, late spring gets tips up (right).

A GOOD JUMP

Here's a good jump by a seven-year old boy, who lands at about 15 meters (about 50 feet). His inrun position is supple and stable (1) and he seems to be a natural in the air (7).

But there's lots of room for improvement. Note:

- The spring starts early and is slow, not explosive (3-4).
- From a good start, with weight on the whole foot (1), weight shifts back on the heels (3, 4).
- This back weighting results in a slight, but noticeable forward shift of the legs in the early flight (5).
- So he jacks late, which amputates his flight as he feels he is too far over his skis. (8).
- He doesn't use the Telemark landing (10, 11).

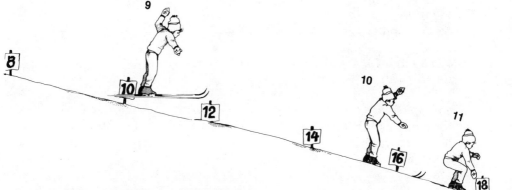

THE JUMPS AHEAD

Very few of the children who learn to jump ever end up as competitive ski jumpers. But many want to maintain and sharpen their jumping skills. Again, the instructor/teacher can be the knowledgeable guide to the terrain that teaches. Go on tours, and seek out opportunities to jump on their downhill stretches. Impromptu jumping skills can come into their own on a mogul-strewn Alpine ski hill. The possibilities are endless, and the thrill of flight is always there to be experienced.

INDEX

(page numbers are manuscript page numbers)

I

Inrun (of ski jump), 28, 152
   position on, 153

J

Jet turn, 134

Jump, jumping
   see ski jump, ski jumping

K

Kick (of stride),
   basic, defined, 32
   characteristics of, 72
   weak, stride, 78
   weak, skate turn, 91

Knees,
   absorbing bumps, 42, 47
   bent, desirability of, 106
   control with, 107
   sink in diagonal stride, 72
   steering skis, 104
   unweighting, 119

Knoll (part of ski jump), 150

L

Landing (in ski jumping), 155
   learning of, 156

Learning,
   basic processes, 22

Learning area, 25
   for cross-country skiing, 66

Learning situation, 36

Lip (of a ski jump), 29

M

Maturity, measures of, 22

Motor skills,
  learning of, 22

O
Outrigger turn, 134

Outrun (of ski jump), 29, 156

P
Play,
  and skiing, 17
  use of in teaching, 23

Plow Christy, 122

Poles, marking,
  characteristics and choice of, 136
  color of, 136, 144
  use of, 40, 61, 111, 117, 118, 136

Poles, ski,
  for basic skiing, 61
  safety tips on, 61

Pole-less skiing, 32

Poling,
  in diagonal stride, 73
  on uphills, 81

R
Readiness, position,
  on downhills, 42, 93

Rhythm,
  importance and use of, 24
  similarity to musical rhythm, 24

Rhythm, stride,
  lack of, 76, 86
  in changes, 86

Roller-coaster dips, 28,
  use of, 47

Rotation, 105,
  as error, 116, 124

Running (error),
  on uphills, 82